Drop Dead

"Open these, please."

"Open?" Mrs. Rundle sounded shocked, but did as she was bid. Paper and ribbon fell from the first gift, revealing a gaudy box. Inside that was a humming-top, and attached to the thread, a card.

"David," said Miss Dykes.

"They're all the same. Just the one word, 'David'."

"Open the rest." She bent to help.

They unwrapped a custom-made watch; fibre-glass skis; a set of Chinese egg-dolls; a set of silk sheets; oil-paint and brushes; moccasins; Bendick's chocolates; and a set of turquoise beads on a chain. Miss Dykes made a list of the articles. As she finished, she looked up to find Mrs. Rundle watching her closely.

"I hope nothing's happened to whoever . . ."

"Nothing," said Miss Dykes curtly. She glanced at the clock in the centre of the hall. "It's late, Mrs. Rundle. I think you should go home now. Lock up carefully, and don't open this strongroom again without my permission. And please don't discuss any of this with anyone." She paused, as if she wanted to confide something more; but the moment passed. She nodded a brisk good-night and headed back across the floor, to the elevator foyer.

Mrs. Rundle was human, and intensely curious; but she had learned not to meddle in what did not concern her. There was no one at home to share a secret. She cooked her supper, took a bath, and went to bed. It was not until she read her newspaper next morning, that she learned she had been on the fringe of a death.

Other titles in the Walker British Mystery Series

Peter Alding • MURDER IS SUSPECTED
Peter Alding • RANSOM TOWN
Jeffrey Ashford • SLOW DOWN THE WORLD
Jeffrey Ashford • THREE LAYERS OF GUILT
Pierre Audemars • NOW DEAD IS ANY MAN
Marion Babson • DANGEROUS TO KNOW
Marion Babson • THE LORD MAYOR OF DEATH
Brian Ball • MONTENEGRIN GOLD
Josephine Bell • A QUESTION OF INHERITANCE
Josephine Bell • TREACHERY IN TYPE
Josephine Bell • VICTIM
W. J. Burley • DEATH IN WILLOW PATTERN
W. J. Burley • TO KILL A CAT
Desmond Cory • THE NIGHT HAWK
Desmond Cory • UNDERTOW
John Creasey • THE BARON AND THE UNFINISHED PORTRAIT
John Creasey • HELP FROM THE BARON
John Creasey • THE TOFF AND THE FALLEN ANGELS
John Creasey • TRAP THE BARON
June Drummond • FUNERAL URN
June Drummond • SLOWLY THE POISON
William Haggard • THE NOTCH ON THE KNIFE
William Haggard • THE POISON PEOPLE
William Haggard • TOO MANY ENEMIES
William Haggard • VISA TO LIMBO
William Haggard • YESTERDAY'S ENEMY
Simon Harvester • MOSCOW ROAD
Simon Harvester • ZION ROAD
J. G. Jeffreys • SUICIDE MOST FOUL
J. G. Jeffreys • A WICKED WAY TO DIE
J. G. Jeffreys • THE WILFUL LADY
Elizabeth Lemarchand • CHANGE FOR THE WORSE
Elizabeth Lemarchand • STEP IN THE DARK
Elizabeth Lemarchand • SUDDENLY WHILE GARDENING
Elizabeth Lemarchand • UNHAPPY RETURNS
Laurie Mantell • A MURDER OR THREE
John Sladek • BLACK AURA
John Sladek • INVISIBLE GREEN

JUNE DRUMMOND

Drop Dead

WALKER AND COMPANY · NEW YORK

All the characters and events portrayed in this story are fictitious.

First published in the United States of America in 1976 by the Walker Publishing Company, Inc.

This paperback edition first published in 1984.

ISBN: 0-8027-3089-2

Library of Congress Catalog Card Number: 75-40759

Printed in the United States of America

10 9 8 7 6 5 4 3 2 1

1

YOU COULD SAY it was the right day for suicide.

The setting was right: a city, massive and almost featureless, slung between steelworks on the east and a few ragged hills on the west. The river that wound across it was so sullied by effluent that it had the pinkish sheen of an earthworm. Industry and railways occupied the left bank, commerce the right. Between the iron-clad earth and a sky puffed with coming snow, lay air motionless, yellow, sour as a tramp's breath.

The season was right: ten days before Christmas, ten jostling, mercenary days before humanity made its annual one-shot attempt at peace and goodwill. At such a season, the direst need is not for gifts, but for inclusion. There must be somewhere to go, some welcome, at least one date with a red circle round it. Those who at Christmas-time have no appointment with the living, fall very easily into conversation with Death.

On this particular evening, the setting and the season being right, Death needed only to walk the streets of the city to find his boon companions.

2

"IN CASH?"

The bank manager sounded startled. He would not have dreamed of challenging the intention of an ordinary client, but he had known this girl from her childhood, was aware of her history and felt some concern for her. She didn't look well, he thought. "That is a great deal of money to carry about in the Christmas crowds, my dear."

"I'm not going to carry it far." The girl's eyes were vague and her speech a little slurred, as if she were too tired to form the words properly. "I'm going to spend it."

The manager said nothing. He glanced at the cheque

on his desk. She wanted to draw two thousand. Christmas shopping? For whom? She had never to his knowledge given a present to a friend, she had no one close to her since her mother died. Some crazy whim? Maybe. The way she lived, that odd apartment down by the river, her painting, her long solitary trips to wild places, must lead her into some strange acquaintanceships.

He felt he should advise her, but her expression forbade it. She was like her father, clever, suspicious, difficult to approach. On impulse he said, "It's been months since we saw you, Ella. Why don't you come and have dinner with us tonight? Marie would like to catch up on your news."

She dismissed the invitation abruptly. "I have other things to do." An impatient gesture. "May I have the money, please?"

Her rudeness annoyed him, so that he did not accompany her to the counter, as he would normally have done.

She drew the money in hundreds, and without checking that it was correct, thrust the wad of notes into the inner section of her handbag. She pushed through the swing-doors into the street. It was just before three o'clock, cold and yet muggy. Traffic was jammed solid in the roadway and a bus belched smoke into her face.

She stood watching for some while, her hands in the pockets of her jacket, her bag swinging carelessly from one wrist. After a while she threaded her way across the traffic-jam and ducked down the steps leading to the underground railway.

3

THE WEATHER BROUGHT the Fifth Mountain Corps into town.

In normal years, there was no snow until late December, and it was mid-January before the falls were heavy enough to allow winter manoeuvres to begin. This year, the foothills were already streaked with white runnels, and the mountains to the north had a cover deep enough to provide good ski-ing.

The Army had decided to make the most of its chances; which meant marshalling a number of soldiers who had formed other plans for Christmas.

Predictably there were some hard feelings, but for the most part morale was good. The Fifth was, after all, made up of men who liked mountains. All of them could ski, or rock-climb, or both; all of them had been hand-picked and given a rigorous training in mountain warfare. They were proud of the fact that each one of them was a specialist. The Corps included crack engineers, bridge-builders, experts in demolition and radio-communication, snipers. Their ability to improvise, to scrounge and survive, amounted to genius. They had mastered the last, most difficult discipline, that of knowing how to combine their skills to maximum effect.

Summoned from depots across the plain, they assembled at regimental headquarters on the south side of the city. At noon the troops began to entrain for Mortimer, the foothill terminus where they would change to the narrow-gauge railway that would take them up past the snow-line. By three-thirty the only members of the unit left in town were Sergeant Henry Coggin and five others.

Coggin was thirty-four years old, a lanky Canadian from Kelowna. Born in a construction camp in the Rockies, he claimed to have Indian blood, which he said gave him his head for heights. He had spent five years repairing bridges at high altitudes, notably in the Alps, and had been a regular soldier for the past eleven years.

At the moment he was in charge of three truck-loads of special equipment that would go north by road, overnight. He was waiting to take delivery of other items that had been delayed in transit, and would not reach the city until seven o'clock. This gave him and his men an awkward wait of three and a half hours. The equipment and trucks could not be left unguarded, and there seemed little point in taking them back to headquarters.

Coggin decided to make for the Methodist Mission.

This was not such an odd decision as it might sound. The Mission was bang in the middle of the main shopping area, the Methodys having clung to their territory despite continuous assaults by land-hungry commerce and certain avaricious city fathers. The building, a three-storey eyesore of red and yellow brick, faced onto Manning Lane between the huge bulk of Kuper's General Store and the Parity Parkade.

It had been run for the last decade by a man named Barry Teale, a wiry little ex-paratroop chaplain with the single-mindedness of an ant-eater. Teale held the simplistic view that what most people wanted was good cheap food, a clean bed, and someone to talk to; and that if one's religion did not express itself in one's own life, then there was no point in talking about it. He had turned the Mission from a rather snivelling institution with a load of debt, into a going concern, billed by both laymen and clergy as the best pad in town.

Coggin swung down from the cab of the leading truck just as Teale was mounting the Mission steps. Teale waited for the soldier to come up with him.

"So Sergeant, you're back. The canteen's open. Snacks only, though, it's a bit early yet."

"We've time to kill, Mr Teale. I wonder, could we park the trucks in the yard? Then a couple of us can keep an eye on them while the others go off for an hour or so."

"By all means. Drive 'em in under the arch and put 'em right up in the top corner, will you?"

"Thanks, sir. I'll be in for a cup of coffee."

Coggin saw the trucks in, set two men to guard them, and told the other three they could scarper as long as they were back by seventeen forty-five. He went into the canteen and drank his coffee, while Teale sat chatting to him. When the minister went off, Coggin moved to the common-room. He found a comfortable if dilapidated armchair, pulled a Datsun 1600 manual from his pocket, and settled down to read.

4

KUPER'S GENERAL STORE was more than a hundred years old. It began life as Kuper's Emporium, a two-storey building with iron-scrolled balconies and a solid teak door, near the old Fish Quay on the river. By the turn of the century, it was so much too small for its trade that a new site had to be acquired in the developing commercial complex further north. The modern Kuper's General Store was established in the 1930s, and there had been extensive additions and interior alterations since that time.

The main entrance doors lay on the northern side, on Parade Square. (Fountains, grass, and a statue of Ebenezer Aberfoyle, Esq., clutching a top hat to his bosom.) On the east side, Porters' Way, once the domain of ships' chandlers, still afforded a short-cut from the river wharves to the municipal vegetable- and meat-markets. Behind the shop, on the south, lay Manning Lane, a narrow street taken up almost entirely by multi-storey warehouses. The underground railway ran beneath these, and the Manning Lane Station was an enormous asset to Kuper's custom. The store was bounded on the west by a vast new Parkade, and the Methodist Mission.

On this particular Wednesday, the Christmas shopping fever was near its crisis, though not yet in the delirium of the final few days. Dazzled by giant mobiles, deafened by a thousand stereophonic sleighbells, the crowds thronged the pavements and surged through every shop-door.

Mr Ernest Smail, Chief Buyer for Kuper's Men's Department, watched the crowds and gloated.

"Better than last year," he told a subordinate, "much better. Our sales will be up by at least five per cent."

The other was misanthropic. "We shall lose one per cent of our entire stock to pilferers."

"The discount houses will lose ten per cent."

"Ah yes, but what they take is through the till, almost pure profit. No accounts, no top-heavy Management, no fancy executives eating their heads off. If we worked that way we could get rid of the top four floors of this building."

"And half our sales staff. Kuper's doesn't have to worry about any trashy bazaar competitors. We have the better type of custom here, our people want quality and service and they get it. If we were to merge with one of the discount houses, you could say goodbye to all that."

"Who's talking about merging? I merely pointed out..."

"...And I'll ask you another question. Where are you going to do your own Christmas buying? Where will you get the best credit, the best rake-off? Here, or over the road?"

"Well, I work here...."

"And the Management doesn't forget it. We look after our own, here, so let's have a little more loyalty, and not so much slipshod talk about matters of which you know nothing."

Mr Smail hipped away towards Sportswear. The junior, staring after him, wondered what was eating the old bee. Probably the weather. Cold weather got him in the bladder, and anyway he was always touchy about Management, thought they were God and you mustn't say a thing against them or the skies would fall.

The fact was, Christmas was hell for the poor bloody shop-worker, and the best thing to do was follow the old army rule; look after your feet and never volunteer, not even an effing opinion.

At least one of Kuper's employees was having the time of her life. Miss Jane Bell, sixteen years old and engaged as a temporary assistant over the Christmas rush, liked everything about her job. She liked her weekly wage-packet. She liked the Gift-Wrapping Department and her immediate boss, Mrs Rundle. She liked the shop. Jane was a worshipper of her own times. To her Kuper's, its caverns booming piped music, its vaults tawny with gilt motifs, its altars loaded with the most rich and splendid offerings, was a holy place. On her first day of work at the beginning of December, she watched the decorators hoist huge golden bells that turned gently in the over-heated air. The sight filled her with awe. She might have been watching the elevation of the Host.

The crowds that lapped and flowed about her were a constant delight. They, like Jane, were pilgrims to the shrine and her sharp little brown eyes devoured them, her sharp young mind stored up all she saw and heard, for future recounting to her peers.

The Gift-Wrapping Department provided her with an excellent window on the world. Kuper's management understood that the sight of gifts being wrapped whets the appetite of buyers in exactly the same way that blood excites sharks. Therefore the wrapping was done in a huge glass tank in the centre of the ground floor. Inside the tank, girls worked at counters laden with brilliant paper, with ribbons and trinkets, tinselled cards and satin-striped boxes. Behind them, the hoist-lifts brought an endless flow of goods from the upper floors. Most of these, once they were in their fancy-dress, went off to a delivery section, there to be veiled in plain brown paper and bundled into vans; but a number were marked for personal collection, and these were arranged on special shelves at the north end of the tank.

This was Jane's realm. Here she sorted and stacked; watched the watchers and, since the tank was far from sound-proof, listened to a good deal of their conversation.

After a few days, she began to play a secret game. She studied the articles coming down on the lifts, and tried to visualise what sort of person had bought them. She imagined faces and forms, and compared these figments of imagination with the real people who later came to her counter. Often her guesses were surprisingly accurate. Sometimes, more amusingly, she was way out. Who would have thought, for instance, that the wife of the Episcopalian Bishop would choose to give him Ten Great Hits of Fats Waller? Or that the old lady who sold Finnegan's Turf Guide outside the Parade Square public house could afford, let alone want, a rock crystal eagle costing over six hundred? Made you think the old girl's tips were probably worth more than Mr Finnegan's.

The game caught on with the wrappers. They began watching out for specially interesting gifts, and telling Jane about them.

So they couldn't help noticing Davey-boy.

Not that that was his real name. Jane used it, and it stuck. Everyone in the department knew about him.

Things started coming down for him at half past three on Wednesday afternoon. The first was a man's wrist watch from Brouard of Paris. It had two sets of straps, one platinum, the other blond antelope. Soon after there followed a set of papier-maché dolls, made in Hong Kong. You unscrewed the first at the waist, and inside was a second, smaller one, until you had a little man less than half an inch tall. Over the next two hours arrived: a tube of Veridian Green oil-paint and two thick brushes; a pair of silk sheets, with pillowcases, for a double bed; a humming-top; moccasins made of reindeer-skin; a box of chocolates from Bendicks of Mayfair; and a set of uncut turquoise stones on a silver chain, which Mrs Rundle said were Greek worry-beads.

"There's no pattern to it," said Jane, watching the beads being tucked into a heart-shaped box. "You can't see what's in her mind, at all."

"Could be his mind," said Mrs Rundle.

"No. A man wouldn't have bought the sheets." Jane considered. "Not unless that David's a queer."

Each article arrived downstairs accompanied by one of the store's own gift-cards. On each card was written, in a spindly, sloping hand, the single word, 'David'. Nothing more, no message of love, no greeting, no hint of the giver's identity. Just before closing-time the last package was wrapped. Fibre-glass skis, for David.

"Lucky swine," said Jane. "She's spent a fortune on

'im, know that? Loves 'im no doubt. Wonder what she's like?"

"Rich," said a wrapper.

"Old?" suggested Jane.

"You can't tell that."

"A rich old woman, keeping 'im in sinful luxury."

Mrs Rundle overheard. "You're too young to talk that way, my girl, and don't let me hear you telling tales or naming names outside of this tank, or you'll be in dead trouble. The customer is sacred, you understand?"

Jane nodded, but she was determined to get a good long look at David's benefactor.

She scanned every face that approached her counter. She kept a jealous eye on the gifts stacked under Number 121, terrified they might be handed over while she was at the far end of the tank. As six o'clock drew near, she became aggrieved.

"Thought they were supposed to collect the same day?"

"If they don't," said Mrs Rundle, "no matter. Everything left goes into the centre safe. The door's solid steel. It'll all be here in the morning."

"But I might miss seeing her."

"Not if you're here on time."

At five minutes to six, everything from the shelves, including the parcels under Number 121, was locked away for the night.

5

THE GIRL STOOD in front of a looking-glass. Her hands buried themselves in the collar of a karakul coat, slowly turning it up round her throat. Her chin moved from side to side, gauging the texture of the pelt. Her eyes closed.

She was not pretty. Her make-up had worn off, and the planes of her face had a waxy shine. Floss-pale hair fell in strands across her forehead. Her shoulders were high and thin, giving her a look of petulance. Yet people turned to stare at her. There was an absorbed purpose in her, she shone like a moth intent upon some unseen lamp.

Watching her, the saleswoman grew uneasy; leaned forward and touched the thin wrists crossed beneath the throat. "Madam? We close in ten minutes."

The girl opened her eyes. Without glancing at the saleswoman she unfastened the front of the coat and swung it wide, groping for the price-tag at the armpit. Her head twisted sideways as she read the mark. She set a sling bag on the counter, reached into it and produced a plastic buying-card. Slowly she pushed the card along the counter.

The saleswoman peered at it without picking it up. "You work here?" Her eyes travelled over the girl, noting the pink French tweed suit, the soft Italian leather shoes. Shop-assistants didn't dress that way, didn't buy silver karakul at one-thousand-twenty-five. "I said, do you work here?"

A finger, thin and delicate, the nail bitten right down, stabbed at the card, pointing to the words 'Art Department'. The saleswoman hesitated. Some of the artists in Kuper's did very well for themselves. Still, it was a lot of money. "I'm afraid," she said, "that over the thousand mark, we have to have a cheque. You still get the store discount for employees, the accountant will see to it."

For the first time, the girl looked directly at the other woman. Her eyes, greenish-blue, sharpened with a contempt that was almost boredom. She shrugged out of the coat, swung it onto the counter, reached into her bag for a second time and pulled out cheque book and pen. Steadily, in a pointed script, she wrote a draft for the total amount. She crossed it, tore it out, and flicked it sideways along the counter.

The salewoman gathered it up and carried it with the card to the cash-desks in the centre of the showroom.

"Over there," she said quietly to the cashier. "That fair girl. You know anything about her? There's something funny...."

She glanced back across the display area. The girl was not paying any attention. She had turned to face the counter and stood leaning both elbows on it. Her head was lowered so that only a half-moon of silvery hair showed above her hunched shoulders.

The cashier checked the signature on the buying-card. "It's all right, love. This isn't her first purchase, she's been buying all over, just about every floor. We rang the office. She works here all right, Christmas temporary, though God knows why if she can afford karakul. Look, if she wants to be the big spender, that's her worry."

"Well, is it? I mean, she might be.... I don't know. She seems queer, somehow."

"She has the cash. I've told you. She's rich, she wants the coat, you wrap it up, wish her a Merry Old Christmas and put the commission in your piggy bank. What's hard about that?"

"Nothing, with three kids."

"All right then. I'll keep her card now, shall I? Sales are closed so it can go straight through to Accounts for discounting, and she can pick it up tomorrow."

On her way back, the saleswoman considered a question: what do you call a fellow-worker who's just handed you a fat fifty in store commission? Madam, or Love? But facing the girl she was filled with unreasonable resentment, and merely said, "Will you take it with you, or shall we deliver it?"

"I'll wear it."

"It's going to snow. The pelt will spoil."

The girl's answer was a chuckle that was somehow more disquieting than her rudeness.

6

"IF IT WOULD snow!" said the woman at the window, and squeezed her eyes shut, as if by doing so she could transform the entire scene. She pressed her right hand into the dark velvet of the curtains and saw in her mind mountains singing, with pines in the sun. She opened her eyes and stared through the glass at greyish lawns and sparse, skeletal trees.

The man in the wheelchair spoke. "Go now, Chris. We'll look after things here."

She turned towards him. She had an arresting face, the forehead high, the jaw a little too prominent, so that the lower lip seemed out-thrust. But this look of scowling concentration softened a little as she answered the old man.

"I can't go now."

He didn't argue with her. He knew she would not leave him before Christmas. He suffered from emphysema, his lungs were like old sponges, without resilience. Even air was too heavy for them. When the illness first started to alter the pattern of his life, he spoke to her. "I am not a cripple. I'll probably live for years. I shall retire from the Board soon, but I shan't lose interest in it, and there'll be plenty to occupy my time. Later on, if I need nursing, I'll get it without battening on my family. In the meantime, there's some new do-it-yourself breathing-machine. I've ordered one."

"The Bird?"

"You've heard of it?"

"Yes. Dr Clemens described it to me."

The machine helped, but it couldn't arrest the disease. Often he urged her to move. "Dave can transfer to the coast," he told her, "it will be good for him and for you, too. You've your own lives to lead."

"He wouldn't go. He'd think you were trying to displace him."

"That's hardly fair, is it? I didn't make him join the firm. He did so of his own choice. I've given him advice when he asked for it, but I certainly haven't put pressure on him, despotic father is hardly my rôle. Does he really have grounds for resentment?"

"It's not exactly resentment."

"What, then?"

"Oh ... sometimes he gets uptight. For example, he

thinks you should have nominated him to the Board instead of Roches."

"I considered it very carefully. If I'd nominated him, the idea would have gone about that he was only elected because I pushed him. In fact, he's one of the best marketing men we've had in twenty years. He'll make the Board on his own merit in a year or two."

"Would he still make it if we moved to the Coast?"

Arnold shrugged. "Perhaps not. There'd be compensatory factors. You'd have your own home. How much longer do you want to be cooped up with your in-laws? I'd have thought a year was more than enough?"

Yet three years later, though David was on the Board and the young Kupers had a penthouse two blocks away, they still spent a good deal of time in the old house. When David was away on business, Christine often moved back into her rooms there.

Arnold had stopped talking about transfers. His illness was becoming acute. On some nights, his struggle for breath was so terrible one felt there was a demon in his room. No one could rest in its presence. The professional nurses were sometimes a necessity, but Arnold hated them. He preferred, whenever possible, to let Christine help him. Sometimes he knew he was driving her beyond her strength, that she longed for the open air, for the solitude and strenuous exercise she loved. She had been a ski-champion until a bad femoral fracture put her out of competitive sport. One of her first purchases after her marriage to Dave, was a shack in the mountains fifty miles away.

From time to time, Arnold was torn by conscience and urged her to get away, take a holiday. Always she gave the same answer, "I can't leave at the moment," and always the words filled him with relief.

She smiled at him now. "I'll take the New Year break, I promise. By then you'll be ... where?"

"Corfu, I suppose."

"Soaking up the sun."

"Yes."

She stepped behind his wheeled chair and pulled it back from the window bay, swivelled it round and pushed it across the room until it was some five yards from the hearth. A fire burned there. The smoky scent was bad for his breathing, but he had an emotional feeling for fires and fought against using electric heaters.

"Put on a couple more logs, Chris."

She did so, laying them carefully across the embers.

"Once," said Arnold, "I had the princely experience of burning cedar. An old tree came down, on the farm. It wasn't fit for the mill, so we used it for firewood. A marvellous aroma."

Christine had not sat down, but remained at the mantelpiece, watching flames spurt from the logs. She knew that tonight, for some reason, he needed to talk, and talk was the last thing she wanted. She wanted to ... burst, scream, run away ... yet you had to fill silence, silence was so dangerous.

"What?" she said, turning towards him.

"I didn't say anything."

"Yes, you did. Something about the farm."

"I spoke of a cedar tree. Christine, is anything...?"

"Why did you leave that place? You all loved it, didn't you? So why did you leave it?"

He blinked, trying to catch up with her leaping mind. "That? Oh, it was impossible for us to stay. Something that Deirdre did. Sometimes, you know, a single event changes everything in a few minutes. Why do you ask?"

"David mentioned having to move. He seemed very bitter. He's never talked about the farm before."

"He was a child. Perhaps because of that, he suffered more. He hated coming back to town. As a matter of fact, we made his schooling the excuse. Perhaps he saw through that, he was always very perceptive." Arnold paused, as if he wondered whether to say more, and then he appeared to change his mind. He reached into the pocket at the side of his chair, drew out a book bound in dark blue suède and held it up.

"Elegant, isn't it?"

Christine went over and took the book from him. She glanced at the spine. Title, SKYROS. Below that, Deirdre Kuper, and below that again, the imprint of a famous publisher. She leafed over the pages. Eight stories. One or two names seemed to recur in several of them.

"Have you read it?"

"Yes."

"What's it about?"

"Various people, in a Greek waterfront café."

"So this time, the victims aren't our friends?"

He sat silent, his right hand moving up to press against his rib cage. She knew she should control herself, but anger boiled up and fumed over. "I suppose the critics will rave about it. I don't call it clever, to watch people, and then use them."

"She doesn't use them deliberately. It's simply that her life, everything she experiences and therefore everyone she meets, is the raw material on which she works."

"With a flensing-knife."

"She's one of the few great living writers of short stories."

"She's a nut. Day after day upstairs in her room, and then off without warning to some crazy part of the world. She doesn't consider you."

"She does, in her way."

"Oh Arnold. You're far too tolerant of her nonsense."

"No. She's the tolerant one in this household."

As Christine's head jerked up, Arnold met her gaze. "Deirdre may dissect, but she never condemns."

"Meaning that I do?"

"Meaning that practically everyone in the world does."

"Perhaps, having no moral sense, she's incapable of making a judgement."

"No," he said again, "don't fall into that mistake. Her standards are quite different from yours or mine, but she has them, and adheres to them very strictly. She has no kindness as you know it, no mercy, but she has insight. That means she does less harm than most people."

"And yet you blame her for that time, on the farm..."

"Not any longer. It was long ago. It's forgotten."

"Is it?" She became aware of the book in her hand, and dropped it back into the pocket of his chair. "When did it arrive?"

"Late yesterday, by special delivery. David was here and took it up to Deirdre. She gave it to me this morning."

"Does that mean she's back in circulation?"

"Presumably."

Christine swung round and marched to the door that led to the dining-room, opened it and leaned through. Coming back, she said, "Four places laid. That's the first time we've been honoured in five weeks. What's happened?"

Arnold shook his head. "I was hoping you could tell me." He bent forward, watching her earnestly. "Chris, where's David?"

"I don't know."

"Has he gone out of town?"

"He didn't tell me he was going anywhere."

"What time did he leave home?"

She shrugged. "I was asleep."

"So you don't know his plans?"

"I've told you!"

Arnold lifted a deprecatory hand. "I don't mean to pry. It's just that he wasn't at the store at all, today. I 'phoned to remind him to bring the Christmas champagne. Marion Dykes said he hadn't been in. She was surprised because they'd fixed to meet this morning."

"You know Dave. He does what he likes, when he likes."

"He doesn't skip appointments, as a rule. I suppose ... you didn't have a row last night?"

"Of course not!" Her fair skin flushed with furious colour. "Has someone been saying things about me?"

"No, no." He leaned back, tucking in his chin, his skin suddenly grey and clammy. Christine's anger vanished and she ran to his side.

"Oh my dear, I'm so sorry. I didn't mean to tire you. Nothing is wrong, I promise. Would you like a rest before dinner? There's plenty of time. I'm sure Dave won't be home till at least half past seven."

He nodded, signalling that he would like to go upstairs to his own room. She wheeled his chair along to the lift that had been installed for him at the rear of the house. As they passed through the central hall, they saw Deirdre coming down the stairs. She was walking very slowly, reading something on the inner pages of the evening newspaper.

7

AT FIVE-THIRTY, THE long sets of electronically-operated doors on Kuper's flanks were set at 'Exit Only', and the staff began to herd out lingering customers. By five-forty, the sales floors were cleared, and the sales personnel beginning to pour through the staff exit into Porters' Way.

Jane Bell was one of the first to leave, her white angora beret bouncing through the rush-hour crowds like a rabbit's rump. Ernest Smail left more sedately, having taken time to put on a black pure-wool top-coat, a pair of fur-lined boots, and a hat trimmed with astrakhan. In private life Mr Smail was something of a dandy. He believed in displaying Kuper's wares as widely as possible. The Russian style hat was both practical and dashing and was selling very nicely.

Under his right arm, Smail carried two large folders of manufacturers' brochures. The increased Christmas sales, satisfactory though they might be, were no more than a vindication of decisions taken by the buyers eighteen months ago. Tonight, he intended to sit at home over a good fire and focus his mind on the trends for 1976.

He turned left in Porters' Way, emerged into Parade Square, turned left again and walked along the block. At each of Kuper's windows he stopped to study the display. He was really very pleased. The dressers got better every year. They had the advantage of improved materials, of course. Marvellous what could be done with plastics, and the dummies were works of art, well worth the money spent on them.

His bonhomie endured until he reached the far end of the building. There, as always, he was offended by the presence of the Sizzle discount house. Music blared through a dozen still-open doors, and its flat glass front revealed swarms of people clogging the turnstiles within.

Mr Smail's mouth grew prim with distaste.

Gimcrack, in his opinion. He'd made a point of going to see their Christmas lines. Shoddy stuff, a lot of it with flaws or imperfections an experienced eye could pick up at a glance. Mr Smail remembered a jacket marked 'wool' that was certainly a mixture of woollen and synthetic fibres. That was a deliberate infringement of the law. His own top-coat now, was Italian, cheaper than the British but still very good, and well within the means of the poor fools being fleeced by Sizzle's robbers.

He turned back to Kuper's. Despite what he had said to young Verity that morning, he did not take lightly the competition of the discount houses. He had seen too many of the old names go down before them, beautiful shops with distinguished records absorbed and turned into circuses.

There was talk. It reached his ears, not as outright statements which could be challenged and refuted, but as rumours and smears. Take-over, they said, was looming closer, and some of Kuper's top men were protecting their own positions in dubious ways. Really, the world was becoming a very unpleasant place. The worst aspect was its brazen dishonesty. Sly methods were considered smart. There was an air of betrayal everywhere.

Mr Smail began to feel chilled. He shouldered across the pavement and entered the Parkade where he kept his car. Here again he paused. He had been meaning for days to call at the Methodist Mission. He was a solid church-goer and the minister, Barry Teale, was an old friend. It would do him good to talk to Barry, and it would be a chance, perhaps, to show his brochures to the youngsters in the canteen and get their reactions.

Accordingly, he walked through the Parkade and emerged next door to the Mission. Its windows had red and white cotton curtains and the light shining through them was most cheerful. One set of curtains on the ground floor had been looped back and a modernistic Christmas tree stood on the ledge between them. Beyond it a large group of young people were dancing. From the basement there rose a powerful smell of brown stew and hot coffee.

Mr Smail marched briskly up the steps and rang the doorbell.

Not all of Kuper's employees got away on time. Mrs Rundle, for instance, stayed to tidy up the Gift-Wrapping Department. Being a widow without children, she had no urge to hurry home, and the overtime she earned would go towards next year's holiday. She planned to visit the Holy Land, had already saved her fare and was getting together her spending-money. She worked quickly and neatly, enjoying the quiet and space after the noise and jostle of the day.

A surprising number of other people were busy in Kuper's Building. Several lights still burned in the offices on the top three floors. Lower down, in the Mail Order Department, the night shift had just come on duty. In Packaging and Despatch, the Truck Depot and the Parkade, work would continue almost round the clock. Kuper's, like the hospitals and hotels of the city, never really slept, and already there moved through the half-lit corridors and show-rooms a horde of cleaners who must make good the ravages of the day; engineers to check the electrical systems; maintenance men to service the many refrigerators and stoves, air-conditioners and heaters that operated throughout the store.

Between five-thirty and five-fifty, the switchboard operators disconnected most of the internal lines and set the board for the night, leaving access only to a few offices and utility areas.

Over on the east side, the caretaker remained in his day-room next to the staff exit, and would do until eight o'clock. At a quarter to six, he and the full-time Security Officer admitted three extra Phoenix patrol-men with dogs. Over Christmas, extra guards were always engaged. Once checked in, men and dogs dispersed to fixed points in the store.

At six o'clock, a final warning-bell rang, and all public entrances were locked. In his control-room in the basement, the Engineer tripped a switch, setting the Phoenix Emergency Alarm System. Now anyone entering the store in an unauthorised manner would break an electronic circuit that not only triggered a series of automatic cameras at key points throughout the building, but rang buzzers in the security firm's headquarters and in the main City Police Station.

Kuper's was therefore a sealed box. Anyone wanting to leave would have to do so via the Trucks door or the staff exit; unless, of course, he owned a set of Director's keys, which included one to the door connecting with the Parkade next door.

The girl in the fur coat seemed to understand the inner workings of Kuper's extremely well.

Soon after five-thirty, she let herself into the Art Department on the tenth floor. The studio was deserted. She locked the door behind her, moved across to the big north window and stood there for some time, gazing out at the city. The sky was opaque, stained here and there by the reflected glare of neon lights. Once someone tried the locked door. A little later the three telephones shrilled together, a signal from the switchboard that the lines were about to be unplugged. On neither occasion did the girl even turn her head.

At six o'clock, when the alarms sounded for final closing, the girl left the studio and walked along a short passage to big double doors marked FIRE EXIT. She pushed these open, slid through and allowed them to close, waiting for the click that showed they were locked. The escape stairs on which she now stood were stone, uncarpeted and lit by powerful wall-brackets. The girl walked down one flight of steps and stopped on a landing, from which a second flight led down to a narrow doorway.

It was quiet here, the air cold and stuffy. The girl waited, hands deep in the pockets of her coat, bag on wrist. She had been there about seven minutes when there was a sudden movement on the far side of the door, the handle rattled under a testing hand and snapped level again. Steps moved away. The girl glanced at her watch.

Again, silence. After ten minutes, the girl opened her bag, lifted out a ring of keys, chose one, fitted it to the lock and opened the door. She paused on the threshold, listening. No sound came from within, and she moved gently forward, turned and relocked the door.

She was in the Soft Furnishings Department, a huge hall two stories deep that ran from north to south through the centre of the building. The architects of the 1930s had designed it as the store's main restaurant, but eating habits had changed, and shoppers preferred coffee and self-service at the series of Bars on the lower floors.

A gallery ran round all four sides of the room, forming a mezzanine floor, used for the display of antique furniture, glass and pottery. From the rail of this gallery there hung long swathes of brocade and velvet, silk and furnishing tweed. The effect, in the subdued light, was of some Plutonic palace, lofty and splendid, yet cold and devoid of life.

The girl had no eyes for her surroundings. She headed across the showroom with the same blind intensity of purpose that had drawn so many glances to her earlier in the day.

On the south side of the room, a double-branched stairway led up to the gallery. She moved up the left-hand flight. At the head of the staircase were two massive gates, wrought iron backed with plate glass. The girl tested them, and when they did not yield, she once again drew the ring of keys from her bag, chose one and fitted it to the lock. The mechanism was stiff, and she had to use the force of both wrists to turn the key.

The gates swung back.

She looked out at a mock balcony, a little over three metres deep. Most of its ground-space was taken up by the pediments of three huge columns that ran upward from this level, to the roof of the building three stories higher. The edge of the balcony was marked by a wrought iron rail, encrusted with dirt and pigeons' droppings.

In the pallid sky beyond hung an orange disc, the illuminated face of the clock in the Spanfexa Tower, south of the river.

The time it recorded was six-twenty.

8

"DAVID SHOULD BE here," said Marion Dykes. "He said he would be. I can't understand why he hasn't let us know."

Deryk Booth gave her one of the practised, benign smiles he used with good effect on fractious shareholders. "There was a snow forecast this morning," he suggested. "Maybe he's holed up somewhere."

"Hardly." Miss Dykes dismissed the Weather Bureau and Booth's opinions with one downward shake of the cuffs. "If you don't mind, I'll telephone Deirdre. She may have heard from him."

"Do, by all means." Booth knew better than to argue. One did not argue with the oracle. It was better to let her defeat herself by her infuriating dogmatism. He watched her stout figure forge across to the battery of house phones in the corner of his office. She knew how to operate the board, of course. No detail of administration in the entire Kuper complex was outside her scope. Bargain basement, eight floors of sales-rooms, three of stock-rooms, three of office-space; restaurants, canteen, cloakrooms, truck depot, and the Parkade; her memory, prodigious and unrelenting, embraced the lot.

Booth watched her pick up a handset and dial. He was aware of her legend ... how she'd joined the firm as a salesgirl at fifteen, how five years later she was a buyer, how at twenty-two she'd got to her feet at a staff meeting and called the Sales Manager a baboon; how she'd been sacked, proved right by later events, and reinstated; how she'd survived the in-fighting of twenty-seven years, rising all the time; and how, when Arnold Kuper retired, he'd nominated her to the vacant place on the Board.

That was two years ago.

Booth also knew she was rumoured to have been Kuper's mistress. Such tales had no relevance. Dykes had succeeded on her own merits; toughness, and the ability to work sixteen hours a day. Let fools discount her powers. He did not. He used them to his own purpose, just as she used his flair for handling people, a flair she conspicuously lacked. She had that weakness, and one other. She was devoted to Kuper. She was obsessively loyal to his store, his friends and his family, simply because they were his.

Some day, that might be turned to good account. Not yet.

Booth was a tall man, spare-framed except for a slight paunch. His head was handsome, he wore his thick hair rather long to match a thick moustache. A certain redness on the cheekbones gave him a healthy look. His eyes were merry and sly.

He sat back in his wingchair with his hands lightly linked on his chest. From time to time he directed a companionable smile at his secretary, Elaine Bondi. He thought her an excellent girl, good to look at but safely married to a husband she adored. Good with clients, and able to get on with the other girls. Smart enough to bring back the little bits of dirt they let fall about their bosses, yet discreet enough to keep her own mouth shut.

"Deirdre?" Marion was using her most effusive voice. "I'm sorry to bother you again, but has David come in? No? Well, no matter. It's just that we're allocating the clients' bonanzas, and it would be useful to have him with us, but I can check the list with him tomorrow. Yes, if you would. If he's in before seven, I shall still be here. Thank you my dear. 'Bye."

She returned to her chair, sat down and fixed her rather bulging brown eyes on Elaine Bondi. "What is the next name?"

"Knebel," said Elaine, and shifted position, slanting her knees to ease the muscles of her legs. She was fairish, plump, with the thick eyelids and secretive smile of a Flemish madonna. This demure look veiled a nature that was sharply acquisitive. At the moment she was wondering why old Dykes was so on edge. Her mind picked over the gossip of the past few weeks. Everyone said that things were going well, the contracts all filled, new lines selling well, profits up, everything set for a happy Christmas. Yet there was this ... jumpiness. Same with Booth. Watching, all the time.

"What did we do about Knebel last year?" said Miss Dykes.

Elaine glanced at the list on her lap. "A case of Scotch."

"Not worth it."

Elaine drew a neat line through the name 'Knebel'. Now why would they be out of favour? Probably nothing important, but she'd mention it to Sam. He could ask around and find out if the Knebel stock was slipping.

"Who's next?" said Miss Dykes.

"Kraft and Fivelman."

"Yes," said Miss Dykes, "the same as usual." She glanced at Booth. "Deryk, you agree?"

He made a faint, acquiescent movement of one finger. "Why not throw in a bottle of scent for Mrs K? Stay the old dragon with flagons."

Marion Dykes nodded.

They worked on down the list. Booth for the most part was silent. His somnolence seemed to indicate that the matter of trade hand-outs was far beneath his notice. When he did rouse himself to offer an amendment to Miss Dykes' view, she accepted it without question. The minutes passed.

At twenty-one minutes past six, this warm peace exploded into crisis. The alarm buzzer in the corridor set up a strident throbbing, a red light flashed on a panel behind Booth's desk. He began to scramble clumsily to his feet, but Marion Dykes was already at the house-phones, dialling the caretaker's extension.

Elaine Bondi, watching the red light, said, "It's on the ninth."

"Probably another false alarm." Booth came round his desk and stood beside Marion Dykes. She replaced the receiver of the 'phone.

"No answer. The old fool's probably gone dashing to the ninth. No, Deryk, wait." She caught Booth's wrist as he turned for the door. "Phoenix and the Police will notify us if the television shows anything. We must keep our heads."

He muttered something, but did as she bid him. The buzzer stopped its clamour, and the silence that followed seemed endless. When the telephone rang, Marion snatched it up.

"Yes? Rudge! Where are you? Is Bronson with you?"

They heard Rudge's voice, high with anxiety. Marion Dykes listened without interruption. Finally, she spoke. "Yes, I understand. This is what I want you to do. Send Bronson to telephone Phoenix. He can use the show-room 'phone, it's connected. You stay exactly where you are. Don't do anything at all, just stay there until we join you."

She hung up. Booth leaned towards her. "What is it? What's happened?"

"There's someone on the dummy balcony, outside the Soft Furnishings Hall."

His face puckered. "In God's name, why? It's been out of use for years."

Miss Dykes took a handkerchief from her pocket and dabbed at her upper lip.

"Someone, a young woman, has unlocked the balcony doors, gone out there and climbed over the guard-rail. She is now standing on the outer ledge. According to Rudge, she means to commit suicide."

9

"KUPER'S GENERAL STORES," said Marion Dykes in a slow clear voice, "the Manning Lane side. What? On the tenth floor. There's a ledge, about a metre wide. She told the caretaker...."

"Hold it a moment, lady." The Captain of police at the other end of the line beckoned to a Sergeant. Putting a hand over the receiver, he said, "That Area Three Alert. It's not a break-in, it's a suicide bid. Some doll on a tenth-storey ledge, Kuper's General Stores, Manning Lane. That's a one-way running parallel with Parade Square, south side. Get a car over straight away, quietly, no fuss; the driver can stay with it and keep us informed. I want two plain-clothes men ... send Lockval, he's had more experience than the rest, and Milner in case it needs muscle ... let 'em go to the main Manning Lane entrance to the store, and I'll see they have someone waiting to let 'em in."

As the Sergeant moved away, the Captain turned back to the telephone. "Okay, ma'am. We're sending two men over straight away. Their names are Lockval and Milner, and I'd like you to arrange for someone to meet them at the main door on the Manning Lane side. Take them straight up to that balcony, and let them try and talk to the girl. Do what they tell you to, because they've been through this before. Who's with her at the moment?"

"Mr Booth, our Sales Manager, and his secretary, Mrs Bondi. They went straight down. Then there's the caretaker, Mr Rudge, and a security officer from the Phoenix Agency."

"Good. Now, Miss Dykes, a lot is going to depend on what the people on the spot do. We get a lot of practice with these ledge-climbers. Usually they've got no intention of jumping, they just want to call attention to themselves. But you can't take any chances. You must act as if the threat is genuine, see? I'm going to try and get hold of a psychiatrist who's helped us before, his name is Dr Lucas, but until he gets there, it's up to you folks to keep that girl alive. That means keeping hold of her mind. Do anything you can to hold her attention. Keep her talking, keep her watching you, make her yell, or swear, or cry, any damn thing that lets her feel she belongs in the land of the living."

"But if she's already decided to...?"

"She hasn't, or you wouldn't be talking to me. What's she like to look at? Young, crazy, drunk, hopped-up, pregnant?"

"I haven't seen her."

"Well, when you do, take a good look at her. Anything that tells us why she's out there may help bring her in again. Understand, the fact she didn't go up there and jump, means there's something keeping her back. There's some argument in her mind. We have to help her win it.

"Another thing. It's important to keep things quiet. I'll do all I can to stop a crowd from gathering round Kuper's, but sooner or later, someone's going to spot her, and then the game's on!"

"Game? My God!"

"It is, to some people, Miss Dykes. You ever been at the scene of a bad accident? Seen 'em bring the kids to get a good look? Dying's a five-star spectacular to some. I know you don't like those sort of goofers any more than

I do, so please, warn anyone that's still in the store to keep their mouths shut. No 'phoning the Press, no chatting to the neighbours, nothing. I'll instruct the Phoenix Agency to do the same. Keep it quiet as long as you can and the kid's got a better chance of getting off the ledge alive. You understand, there's a certain sort of nut that once they've got an audience ... well ... they feel they can't let their public down."

"Yes. I see. We'll try. Captain, what is your name?"

"Finlander."

"Will you be coming yourself?"

"If I can. First, I want to get Dr Lucas."

"Of course. Thank you. Goodbye."

Miss Dykes found, when she replaced the receiver, that she was trembling from head to foot.

Down at street level, however, there was no such distress. The buzzers had sounded briefly, and now were silent. A few passers-by waited to see what might develop, but as no prowl cars appeared, they soon grew bored. Another false alarm. Happened all the time, that was what you got with these fancy new systems.

They drifted away to the glitter and the music of Parade Square.

10

"SHE HASN'T MOVED, sir. Just stands there lookin' about all the time, as if she doesn't even notice the drop." Rudge glanced from Booth to Elaine Bondi with pleading eyes. "Oughtn't someone to go and talk to her? I mean, that's what you do, innit? Kind of talk sense into them?"

"You take one step out there," said Bronson, "she'll do a dive. She's listening even if she's not looking." He was a youngish, thickset man with curling black hair and eyes so close-set they appeared to squint. From time to time he reached out to touch the head of a German police dog who sat close at his side.

Booth, the two other men, and Elaine Bondi were

standing just inside the two iron gates. Booth edged forward a little to get a clear view of the girl on the ledge. She was standing with her back to the balcony, her arms stretched sideways, her hands looped almost casually over the iron railing. She was wearing a silver-grey karakul coat, no hat. Her head was inclined slightly down, and to the left. Bronson was right, she was listening.

Suddenly fear swept through him. It expressed itself in rage with Rudge. "How the bloody hell did she get in here? What the hell use is security if anyone can get in?"

"Well, sir," Rudge licked his lips, "when the alarm went off, I got straight up to the ninth floor. Bronson was in the foyer with the dog. We checked the floor. The doors were all right and tight, till we come to this one, and we could see right away the gates were open. We came up the steps, and then we saw her out there. On the ledge. I told Bronson to keep an eye on her whilst I ran back to 'phone Miss Dykes."

Booth turned to Bronson. "How, may I ask, did the woman get past you?"

"Never passed me. Never saw her until now."

"Don't be insolent, you know perfectly well what I mean. How does she come to be in the store at all, after closing hours? We pay you considerable sums to see that no one remains behind. How long have you been on duty?"

"I came on at five-forty-five. I brought Cobber with me, took 'im through to the Staff Cloaks so's I could change into my gear." Bronson indicated his black uniform slacks and jersey.

"Had you checked this show-room by the time Miss Dykes rang Rudge?"

"Yuh. Six o'clock, I started my first round on this floor. I reached the Soft Furnishings about six-nine. Tested the emergency door, that's the one on the far side, leads to the emergency stairs. It was locked okay."

"How can you be sure of the time?"

"Looked at my watch."

Bronson's manner seemed to get under Booth's skin.

He began to shout. "I shall have serious complaints to make to your employers. You don't appear to understand that if the girl jumps off that ledge, it is going to do Kuper's a great deal of harm."

"Not gonna do her any good, either, is it?"

"Well, good God, man, naturally the safety of the girl is everyone's first consideration, but it's also my duty to protect Kuper's interests. The police will be here very shortly, and they are going to want to know why security was so lax that not only could a stray suicide stay in the show-room quite undetected, but she could force open these gates without setting off the alarm system."

"That's easy. She didn't stay in, she got in. She had a set of keys, for sure."

"What do you mean?"

"What I say. She let herself in, with a key. And she opened these gates with another key."

"How can you be sure of that?"

"Look, Mr Booth, Cobber was trained by the right people. I took 'im right through this show-room, all round the gallery too. If there'd been anything 'uman hidden anywhere, then Cobber would 'ave known."

"The dog's not infallible, is it? There are a number of places a slip of a girl could hide, aren't there?"

"No," said Bronson, and meeting his contemptuous little black eyes, Booth believed him.

"Very well. Let's take it that she was not in the show-room at six-nine when you entered it, and that she got in after you left. What time was that?"

"Just on six-twenty."

"After which she made her entry?"

"Right."

"How?"

"Through there," said Bronson, indicating the small emergency door on the far side of the show-room. "I reckon she must have waited on the tenth floor, in one of the offices. When the final warning rang, she'd let herself out onto the emergency stairs. You can get through the Fire

Doors, but you can't get back again, because they only operate the one way. She'd 'ave come down the stairs and waited until she heard Cobber and me check this showroom. Once we were out, she'd unlock the door and come in. Like I said, she's got herself a set of store keys from somewhere."

"That's impossible."

"So maybe she's a Japanese conjuror. Or maybe she knows where to lay hands on a set. Got one yourself, haven't you?"

"Certainly, and it's locked in my safe, I assure you."

"Maybe not everyone's so careful."

Booth glared at the security man, but did not contradict him. "Well, you'll have to repeat all you've told me to the police, I've no doubt. I suggest you are careful yourself about accusing others of negligence." A thought appeared to strike him and he turned to the caretaker. "Rudge, when you 'phoned Miss Dykes, you apparently said the girl meant to kill herself. Does that mean she spoke to you?"

"Yes, sir." Rudge frowned, trying to remember the exact event. "We came up the stairs. The doors here were open. Bronson said, 'Watch it, the bugger might be armed.' Because we thought it must be someone broke in. The dog was pulling on his chain, he knew there was someone out there, and a' course as soon as we reached the gallery, then we saw her. She was on the ledge, facing us. She wasn't hanging onto the rail properly, just leaning against it. I said, 'Don't scare her,' and Bronson told Cobber to sit. Then he tried to go out on the balcony, quite slowly, see? But as soon as he set foot through the doors, the girl called out, 'Don't come any further or I'll jump.' I stood beside Bronson and I said something about, 'Don't do anything silly, you've got your life ahead of you.' Well, you can't think of anything clever, at a time like that, can you? I mean, the shock of seeing her, I just thought, we mustn't let her do it.

"She looked at me when I spoke. Her eyes are kind of

... not right. You'll see, if you get up closer. She looks at you as if you don't count for anything. Know what I mean? She doesn't care. I said, 'Please come back inside, we're your friends.' And she laughed. She said, 'I'm going to kill myself. When it snows, I'm going to kill myself.'" Rudge made a helpless gesture. "She means it, Mr Booth. What are we going to do?"

Booth said, "Is there any other way we can reach her, except through those doors?"

"No. There's a kind of buttress on each side of the balcony. The ledge stops there. The three big columns go right up to roof-level, and there's no windows behind them, on any floor. There are windows on the ninth, but they're right under the balcony, and the overhang's at least three metres, maybe more. We can't reach her except from here, and if we try it, she'll jump."

Elaine Bondi, who had been standing a little apart from the others, spoke for the first time. "Her bag is lying on the ledge."

The men stared at her.

"If we could get hold of it," she said, "there might be something in it that would tell us who she is. We could get in touch with her family...."

"No chance," said Bronson. "She won't let you near her."

At that moment, they heard the lift ascending to the main foyer. In a short while, Marion Dykes came through the archway into the show-room, accompanied by two burly men in civilian clothes.

Booth said, "That's the police," and hurried down to meet them, followed more slowly by Bronson and Rudge. Elaine Bondi remained where she was, appraising the girl.

Crazy, she decided. Crazy, but certainly not broke. That fur coat was a good one. The poor kook was going to need it, with the wind in the north. "The north wind doth blow, and we shall have snow, and what will the robin do then, poor thing?" A silver karakul cost money. Money could mean a wealthy family, that would be grateful for any services rendered.

Elaine's little pink tongue crept along her upper lip.

Presently a footfall sounded on the gallery, and she turned to find Marion Dykes at her elbow.

"Has she told us her name?"

"No."

Marion took a tentative step. At once the girl on the ledge spun round like a weathercock.

"Get away from me!"

"My dear, I only want to...."

"Fuck off, you old cow!"

Marion and Elaine retreated to the gallery. Elaine spread her hands. "It's useless. We can't help her."

Marion Dykes was still peering at the girl. "That karakul," she said, "it's one of ours. The line only came in this week, and it's exclusive to us."

"What? Then, if she bought it here..."

"Precisely. Tell Mr Booth, will you, that I have gone to check all sales made in Furs since Monday? I shall have to 'phone Mrs Greenberg. She lives right out at Frampton Heights, but she may just be home by now."

She hurried away. Elaine's face sagged in discontent. She was furious with herself, for missing the point about the fur coat.

II

THE GIRL ON the ledge did not think about death. She was empty of thought. She lifted her head and blew out a plume of breath that vanished on the back of the wind. She was conscious of the people behind her, scurrying and squeaking like mice in a bin, but they did not trouble her. They would do whatever she wanted them to do.

From time to time she bent forward to gaze down the cliffs of darkness. She could see the face of the building, the irregular glow of windows that went out as she watched. Far, far down was a broad band of red, gold and green. Below that, right at the bottom of the canyon, little flakes of colour rolled on a river of light.

He was down there, not loitering but hurrying towards her, arms outstretched and ready.

The girl broke into laughter. She clung with one hand to the rail and leaned far out, swinging her free arm in a wide arc. If she leaned a little farther, she could touch the building opposite. She could reach any thing and any person, pluck them from space, hold them close or drop them down, whatever she liked.

She was immensely powerful.

She began to sing to herself, not a formal song with words, but the steady droning of a child that is certain of happiness.

12

"WHAT'S THAT NOISE?" demanded Deryk Booth.

"She's singing."

"My God!"

"We can be glad of it, sir." The policeman who had introduced himself as Sergeant Lockval turned from the open doorway. "If the acoustics are good, we'll be able to hear everything she says, even if she won't let us out there; and she'll be able to hear us. That's vital."

"What do you plan to do?"

"Could I borrow a chair?"

"Of course."

Bronson ran down to fetch a chair from the show-room. The policeman regarded Booth steadily.

"You're sure you've told me everything, sir?"

"Yes. Sergeant, I must stress that we all feel very badly about this. We take every precaution we can to prevent such things happening."

"I'm sure you do. A suicide can be very determined. Cunning, too. They'll go to endless trouble to set things up, sometimes."

"Do you think she really is suicidal? I mean, if she

really means to kill herself, why hasn't she already jumped? The fact that she's waited ... surely that suggests she's ... well, an exhibitionist who simply wants to draw the limelight?"

"Perhaps. That still doesn't mean she won't jump. Some of them will keep you wondering for hours, and then go. Or you'll pull them out of the river Monday, and Tuesday they'll do it some other way. There's the sort that never says a word to anyone. That kind will kill himself and maybe take his wife and kids with him. Others will go on and on talking about it until nobody believes 'em any more, and then one day it's for real. The aggressive ones are different again. It's like they want to punish us, they want to hit us hard, even if the only weapon they can find is themselves. They want to show us what a dirty, rotten lot we are. This one could be like that. We have to try and find out what's on her mind. When the doctor arrives, very likely he'll give us advice. In the meantime, we must do the best we can."

"You've seen a lot of these cases, have you, Sergeant?"

"Some, sir."

"And how many have actually ..."

"Some, sir. Not all. Now, if you don't mind, I'm going to try talking to her. Milner will stay here, just inside the door. The rest of you, please keep out of sight and don't make too much noise. Let me know directly the doctor arrives."

Lockval took from Bronson the chair he offered, and moved to the doorway. He stood there quietly for a moment, and the image sprang to Booth's mind of a lion-tamer, standing at the entrance to a cage. In the silence, they could hear a steady droning sound, the girl singing to herself.

Lockval set the chair down very gently, on the balcony. Slowly, almost casually, he walked round and sat down. He took a pack of cigarettes from his pocket and lit one. He blew smoke and then said in his deep voice, "What's your name, love?"

The girl went on singing without pause.

"You've chosen a tough night for it, haven't you? Must be cold enough to freeze your arse, out there?"

No answer. Lockval leaned back and crossed his legs. "The weather office says it'll snow, but I'm not so sure. I've lived in these parts all my life, and I never knew it to snow when the wind was due north. It'll have to swing a few points east, yet."

The singing stopped. The girl made a faint, irritated movement of the head.

"Did you leave a note?" said Lockval.

Silence.

"People usually leave a note. I expect you did too. Soon, someone will find it and be pretty miserable."

A hand came up, caught a strand of fine silvery hair, twisted it round a finger.

"Someone will find it, and come over here pretty sharp. That's my guess. But it would be safer to go and meet them, wouldn't it, instead of waiting here? I mean, that note might not get read unless you show where it is? It's easy to miss a note. It can blow away, or someone else might find it and throw it away. That would be a shame, when you've taken all this trouble. I think you should come back inside and tell me where you put it."

The girl turned round with a suddenness that tossed her hair sideways in a wide pale plume. She stood with legs wide apart, one hand thrown up to shield her eyes from the light. The impression was that she peered at Lockval through the spread fingers.

He spoke quietly. "What's your name, love?"

She leaned forward and back, slowly, until her body was inclined at a dangerous angle over space. Lockval took a pull at his cigarette. The white paper was damp with sweat. He blew smoke and the girl slowly pulled herself upright again.

Steadily, keeping his voice level and his eyes calm, Lockval talked. He talked about anything he could think of, anything that might hold the erratic attention of the woman on the ledge. All the time he talked, she kept up her slow swaying, out into empty air, back again; while the clouds sank lower and the storm came closer to the city.

13

At seven-thirty-five, Deryk Booth 'phoned the Kuper household. Christine Kuper took the call, and told him that Arnold was resting.

"He's not at all well, Deryk. He gets so little sleep, I'd rather not disturb him, unless it's urgent."

"It is, I'm afraid. Is Dave home?"

"Not yet." Chris hesitated. There was no love lost between her and Booth, but they were careful not to antagonise each other. "He should be back for dinner. Shall I ask him to 'phone you?"

"Please. Tell him it's an emergency. A girl has managed to get herself out onto a ledge...."

"What?"

"Yes, on the tenth floor. Obviously she's an hysteric, and we expect to get her off in one piece, but I felt I should warn Arnold, before someone else does. I've instructed our switchboard to monitor all calls, no Press or Television people will be allowed to speak to anyone but myself. Still, the story may leak out. Did Dave say where he was going?"

"No."

"Well, ask him to 'phone me as soon as he's back, will you?"

"Of course. Deryk, don't hang up. Are the police there?"

"Yes, and we're expecting a doctor, one of these psychiatric guys who work with Lifeline. Don't worry, I'm sure we'll sort things out."

"Would you like me to come down?"

"No, no. In fact, I think it would be a mistake, at this stage. Too many people know your face, and if you were seen coming into the store so late, it might attract attention. But Dave must come." Booth sounded both anxious and irritated. "There's no need to upset Arnold. He can't do much, so I'll leave it to you and Deirdre to tell him or not, as you see fit."

"I'll tell him when he wakes."

"As you please. Goodbye. I'll keep in touch."

"Thank you."

Christine replaced the receiver and went slowly back to the living-room. Deirdre Kuper was there, curled up on the sofa, a tumbler of whisky and water in one hand. She was a slender woman, even thin, with a high-bridged nose and strongly-marked cheekbones. Her skin was pale and smooth, her hair of that true, rich brown that is rarely seen. By contrast, her eyes seemed strangely light. Their regard was both probing and enigmatic. At the moment she wore brown velvet trousers and a black jersey, the sleeves pushed up to her elbows. Round her right wrist was a bracelet made of jagged twigs of gold. She glanced up as Christine entered the room.

"Who was it?"

"Deryk. 'Phoning from the store." Christine stood in the centre of the floor, her arms wrapped round herself. "I don't trust that bastard. He's against Arnold. Deirdre, have you heard anything? About a takeover by Sizzle's?"

Deirdre looked mystified and Christine shrugged. "Oh, forget it."

"Is that why he 'phoned? About a takeover?"

"No. He's in a stew about a woman who's got into the store. Some lunatic. She's climbed out on a ledge ten floors up and says she's going to throw herself off. Deryk thought Arnold should be warned."

Deirdre's gaze, momentarily intent, dropped to the glass in her hand. She swirled the liquid round gently.

"What's the woman's name?" she said.

14

MARION DYKES WAS also engaged in a telephone conversation. Locked in her own office on the eleventh floor, she listened to the nasal tones of Mrs Wilma Greenberg, head of Kuper's Furs Department. Wilma had joined the store in the same year as Marion, and come up through the ranks with her.

"We sold three of the karakul," she said. "All today. Monday we unpacked them, Tuesday no sales, but today, three. It's the first cold snap, so maybe Poppa's ready to play Santa Claus."

"Did you make any of the sales yourself?"

"One."

"Can you describe the buyer?"

"Sure. Sixty-five years old, twenty kilos overweight, with a red hairpiece I wouldn't pin on a dog. What's the matter, Marion? You trying to tell me there's something wrong with these sales?"

"Not on your side of the counter, Wil, but there is a problem. I have to check the buyers. Did you see either of the other two?"

"Not close. I passed one of their credit cards as okay."

"Was it a Kuper's card?"

"No. Premier Bank."

"And the buyer?"

"Male, executive type, about forty-five, maroon suit, plum-and-white striped shirt. Very smooth."

"And the third?"

"A skinny blonde. Pink and grey tweed suit, probably man-tailored. She was very narrow on the shoulder. She picked the Leda style, you have to be skinny for that one."

"That could be her. Do you remember her name?"

"No. She paid by cheque and it went over to the Accounts Desk for verification."

"What's your ceiling for credit-buying?"

"Two thousand. Or one thousand if the card's one of our own."

"You mean the girl might be an employee?"
"It's possible."
"The cheque was accepted?"
"Yes."
"And the girl took the coat with her?"
"I think so. Listen, Marion, I want to know what's the trouble. It's my Department, I've got a right to know..."
"Wil, I told you there's no cause to worry. What time did the girl make her purchase?"
"Late. Just before closing."
"Who was the saleswoman?"
"Hetty Kannemeyer, I think. I was busy myself, with a customer wanting alterations."
"Is Hetty on the telephone?"
"No. She lives way down on the south side. Her husband left her you know, she has three kids and she had to sell her house. I could drive over and speak to her, if you like."
"Would you do that? Try not to excite her, and impress on her that she's not to talk to anyone."
"So how can she talk? What's she gonna talk about if nobody tells her what's happening?"
Marion Dykes was silent for a short space. Then she said. "I can tell you this much. The girl who bought that coat may be contemplating suicide, and it's imperative to get her name and address, so we can call in her family."
"Suicide? How, suicide?"
"She's standing on a tenth-floor ledge."
"My God. At Kuper's?"
"Yes. Wilma, we can't waste time."
"For sure. I'll get over and talk to Hetty. If she can remember the name, I'll ring you right away. Where can I get you?"
"Soft Furnishings. We're leaving that line open, and I'll be down there."
"You thought about other departments? She could have been buying all over the store."
"I've already asked the Head Accountant to come in.

We'll have to examine any cheques that came through this afternoon and are not yet banked. Also, all purchases made by employees' credit cards."

"That could take hours."

"That's why Hetty might be a short cut."

"I'll ring as soon as I can. 'Bye, Marion."

Mrs Greenberg hung up. Miss Dykes started for the Accountant's Office, further down the corridor. But before she reached it, she changed her mind, and turned back towards the elevator foyer.

15

"WHY DID YOU ask her name?" said Christine.

Deirdre Kuper looked up in surprise. "Isn't that the first thing one wants to know? An anonymous suicide, waiting to die, alone out there in this cold? It's intolerable..."

"No one asked her to use our premises, did they? She hasn't considered us."

"Suicides don't usually give much thought to others."

Christine sat down slowly. "I feel I should be down there, but Deryk says not. And what about Arnold, should I wake him? What do you think?"

"Leave him for the moment. When he wakes, he'll have to know."

"If only he'd left for Europe when I wanted him to."

The room was growing dark, and Deirdre switched on a light. It showed Christine sitting with her head back. Her eyes held a feverish anxiety.

"Chris," said Deirdre, "where's David?"

"How the hell do I know? Working somewhere, playing somewhere. He said he might be late."

"That's rather strange." As Christine glanced round sharply, Deirdre met her eyes. "Yesterday evening, Dave came up to see me in my study. I showed him the new book and he said, 'This deserves champagne.' I said, 'Now?', and he said, 'No, tomorrow. We'll come to dinner. I'll leave work early and bring the fizz with me.' That's why I told Nancy to set the table for four. Of course, he might have changed his mind?"

Christine said nothing, and Deirdre went on, "He was in a very strange mood, I thought. Very tense and excited. It seemed to me he was scheming something."

"Well, he does scheme. He does get excited, and he is capricious. Why build it up into a drama? I mean, it's not unknown for a businessman to find he must change his plans."

"It's a little odd if he skips the office without telling anyone."

"What are you suggesting, Deirdre? That I should start checking up on Dave?"

The older woman stretched out an arm and placed her glass on a side-table. Her eyes were piercingly bright. "I think you should," she said. "I think you should check up on him before it's too late."

Christine rose from her chair and came across the room. "All right. Let's have this out now. What poison have you been swallowing?"

"None. I've made my own observations."

"Spied, you mean! Picked up the dirt wherever you could find it!" As Deirdre made no answer, Christine suddenly threw her hands wide in despair. "Oh, please, I'm sorry. I hardly know what I'm saying, tonight, everything is so ... I'm so sick of ..." She came round the sofa and flopped down on the end of it, hunching forward over her knees. Almost under her breath she said, "I am so dead sick of being shut out. I can't reach him. Do you think he's found someone else?"

"Perhaps."

"He's had affairs, before. They weren't important. They didn't come close to us." Christine's voice was defiant, the voice of someone who must confide in a woman she dislikes.

"But this time," suggested Deirdre, "it's different?"

"Yes. This time, I don't know if there is an affair.

Before, I've always found out quite quickly. Almost as if Dave didn't feel the need to hide it from me. You know, before we were married, he said to me, 'I can't be tied down,' and I said, 'Okay, I won't tie you.' It's worked all right, for me as well as for him. We've been happy."

"And now you are not." Deirdre got up and crossed to the table where the decanters stood, and mixed herself a drink. She stood by the table, sipping. "How's your glass?"

"All right." Christine turned to face the fire, as if she wished to close the conversation, but almost at once swung round again.

"How have we changed?"

"To each other? I don't know. I can only watch from the outside. But there is change. David has changed his friends, for one thing. He used to run with the business set. Now, he doesn't."

"So who, then?"

"I don't know. That's why I'm telling you, find out."

"I won't spy...."

"Oh, stop using that damn childish word. I don't suggest a detective agency, I suggest your own resources. David is as far from you as the Pole Star. Try getting close enough to learn what's on his mind, that's all. If he's drifting away from you, try and catch up with him. It may not work, but try!"

"Do you think I haven't tried? You're so arrogant!" The younger woman's face was set in a belligerent glare, the lower lip out-thrust, the fair brows contracted into one straight bar. Deirdre suddenly smiled. "Chris, you look exactly as you did the first time I saw you, at the start of the 1967 Downhill. Am I as great an opponent as Devil's Valley?"

"Don't be ridiculous."

"Why don't you go up there after Christmas, and watch the trials? Dave would enjoy it."

"I'll be at the shack."

"Alone?"

"Dave can come if he wants to."

Deirdre returned to the sofa. "He'd prefer Devil's Valley. He likes the ski-ing crowd."

"I've already made all my arrangements...."

"Chris. You asked me how you've changed. One of the ways is about the shack. You bought it for yourself, sure, but that used to mean having your friends there, and certainly sharing it with your husband. Now it's a retreat. Do you think Dave doesn't feel that? You say you feel shut out, but you shut him out, as well."

"I do not!"

The two women sat staring at each other for a moment, and then Christine said in a flat voice, "There is nothing wrong between Dave and me. We sleep together, we understand each other, we still have a good marriage."

"I wonder whether you still have a marriage at all. My guess is that some time between leaving this house, last night, and the time he left for work this morning, you and Dave had a flaming row. I don't think you have the faintest idea where he is now or when he'll be back. I think that he is probably a lot to blame, because he's treated you badly over the years, he's immature, he has certain faults that must make him bloody difficult to live with. But you are also to blame."

Christine's cheeks and eyes sparkled with anger but she spoke in a level voice. "Okay, tell me how."

"You have made Arnold the centre of your life."

"That's not true." Anger gave way to panic. "Arnold needs me. He needs me because he's ill, I'm a companion to him, a friend, I give him the things you should give him and don't. You're so busy writing pearls of wisdom, jaunting about all over the place, you're no help to him yourself and because I want to help him.... What sort of wife are you to him, and what sort of mother to David?... you're utterly cold...."

"Wait. Hush, and listen to me. I know Arnold needs you. I know I am no help to him. I can't be, because I haven't got what Arnold wants. I have no compassion, or very little. I hate sickness. If I had his disease, I'd kill myself quickly. Business is nothing to me, money is nothing to me. So I accept that Arnold takes from you what I cannot provide. That doesn't alter the fact that he has become the centre of your life. He is the only person who really matters to you. Arnold makes that place for you where you are truly at home, most truly yourself. It's him you love, not David."

"I love them both, in different ways."

"You love Arnold in the only way you can love, which is totally. He has the whole of your mind, and if you haven't slept with him, it's only because he's too ill and frail. You sleep with your husband and you think of mine. It's the oldest whore's trick in the world. You call me arrogant. I'm not. Nothing you do can touch me because I simply do not feel it, but David is dear to me and I won't stand by and watch him destroyed."

"You're evil."

"Ah," Deirdre gave a great cry of despair, "if only I could make you understand, if you'd just look squarely at the truth, for once. A few minutes ago I said, go after David. If you'd chosen to do that, I'd have helped you. I'd never have spoken. But it's clear you can't. So I say now, take Arnold. Take him away somewhere, care for him, love him, live your life. I will be grateful, I will bless you for it, believe me."

"You hate me."

"No, no I don't." Deirdre put out a hand, just brushing the girl's sleeve. "But this impossible situation can't go on. In three weeks' time, Arnold will leave for Corfu. Will you do as I ask? Go with him?"

Christine shook her head wildly; but whether she was refusing to leave, or to listen, it was impossible to tell. After a short time, Deirdre turned away, went through to the dining-room and removed one place-setting from the table. When she came back to the drawing-room, it was empty.

16

MARION DYKES WAS crossing the ground floor of Kuper's. Usually she enjoyed a private stroll through her miser's hoard. Tonight she spared it not one glance.

Most of the lights on this level had been extinguished, but there was a pool of brilliance over Gift-Wrappings. Marion could see someone moving behind the glass; that senior assistant, fattish, hair done up on top, what was her name? The woman saw her and came across to open the outer door.

"Don't come through," said Miss Dykes. "I'll join you. You are Mrs Rundle, aren't you? You're working very late."

"There was so much tidying to do. It's quieter after hours, one gets through so much more."

"Don't apologise. I thank God you're here. We have a crisis, Mrs Rundle. Have you seen any unauthorised person on this floor since closing?"

"No. The guards came round, soon after six. I said good evening. They ... they said hello, you know."

"Did they stop?"

Mrs Rundle's neck went red. "Well, yes. The fact is, I always save my tea biscuits for the dogs. They don't eat them down here, of course, that's never allowed, but Dicky Martin who's our floor-guard takes them away for later. I hope you don't think..."

"I'm fond of dogs." Miss Dykes smiled her bleak smile. "Can you recall anyone else beside the guards?"

"Not since the doors shut."

"I see." Miss Dykes thought a moment. "During the day, did you by any chance hand over parcels to a thin, very fair girl, rather bony features, narrow shoulders, pale skin and a nervous manner? She might have been wearing a karakul fur coat. Can you remember anyone like that?"

"I'm afraid not."

"No matter, then." Miss Dykes started to turn away. It was upon that moment that Mrs Rundle, who for all her stodgy aspect was a woman of imagination, was prompted by the gods. She said suddenly, "There was one thing..." Miss Dykes swung round and stared at her. "It was probably nothing important..."

"What?"

"Well, someone bought a lot of gifts and sent them down for wrapping, but never collected them. They must have been bought on a credit card."

"Then you have the number of the card on the dockets?"

"Oh certainly. In here." Mrs Rundle was already making for the inner office, one hand drawing a key-ring from her pocket. "I lock all left articles away at night, in the strong-room."

She unlocked the heavy door and opened it. The room was not large. Shelves ran round three sides, and on these were arranged glittering piles of wrapped parcels. Miss Dykes was astonished at the number. "All these?"

"Despatch will take a lot tomorrow. But these," Mrs Rundle indicated the largest stack, "simply weren't collected, and I have no forwarding address. If they aren't picked up tomorrow, I shall refer to Accounts for advice."

"What's the credit number?"

Mrs Rundle shifted a parcel and pulled out a sheaf of dockets. "Seven-two, point one-nine-three."

Mrs Dykes held out her hand. "I think I'll have those. I'll give you a receipt." She scrawled the docket numbers, added some words, signed and dated the note. Then, gazing at the parcels, she appeared to reach a snap decision. "Open these, please."

"Open?" Mrs Rundle sounded shocked, but did as she was bid. Paper and ribbon fell from the first gift, revealing a gaudy box. Inside that was a humming-top, and attached to the thread, a card.

"David," said Miss Dykes.

"They're all the same. Just the one word, 'David'."

"Open the rest." She bent to help.

They unwrapped a custom-made watch; fibre-glass skis; a set of Chinese egg-dolls; a set of silk sheets; oil-paint and brushes; moccasins; Bendick's chocolates; and a set of turquoise beads on a chain. Miss Dykes made a list of the articles. As she finished, she looked up to find Mrs Rundle watching her closely.

"I hope nothing's happened to whoever..."

"Nothing," said Miss Dykes curtly. She glanced at the clock in the centre of the hall. "It's late, Mrs Rundle. I think you should go home now. Lock up carefully, and don't open this strongroom again without my permission. And please don't discuss any of this with anyone." She paused, as if she wanted to confide something more; but the moment passed. She nodded a brisk good-night and headed back across the floor, to the elevator foyer.

Mrs Rundle was human, and intensely curious; but she had learned not to meddle in what did not concern her. There was no one at home to share a secret. She cooked her supper, took a bath, and went to bed. It was not until she read her newspaper next morning, that she learned she had been on the fringe of a death.

17

"LUCAS," SAID THE dark man. "Dr Simeon Lucas."

He had just stepped out of the elevator, and stood facing Booth with an enquiring look. He was slightly built and his face was narrow, heavily lined, the lips full, the eyes quick and expressive. He was dressed in heavy woollen trousers, a checked shirt, and a sheepskin jacket. A knitted cap was pulled down over his ears.

"I'm sorry I took so long. I was out at Lafitte, I have a clinic there once a week. They caught me just as I was leaving. Where's the girl?"

"Up there." Booth indicated the balcony with a nod, and the two men began to cross the show-room floor.

"Is there anyone else from Lifeline?"

"No. They couldn't find anyone. Seems they all rush off on holiday, and the doctors ... I mean the ones in your line ... are all busy or sick or something."

"There are only five psychiatrists in the city, you know, to cope with a population of close on a million. Who have you got from the Police?"

"A Sergeant Lockval, and Constable Milner."

"Lockval is a good man."

"He's talking to her now, on the verandah."

"I hope he's warmly dressed. These vigils can become endurance tests."

"He has an overcoat on."

"Good."

They climbed the steps. Lucas, glancing round, nodded at a group of two men and two women who were standing further along the gallery, then moved to stand beside Milner. He greeted him softly, introduced himself, and then listened with head bent to the voices beyond the doors. There were two speaking together, the one deep and steady, the other high and erratic. There came the sound of a chair scraping on tiles. At once the woman began to scream.

"Don't you move. Don't come any closer to me. I'll jump."

"I'm not going anywhere. I have to stand up a moment, my leg's cramped."

"I'll jump."

"All right, honey, cool it, I'm sitting down. All I want to do is talk to you, although I could do that a lot more comfortably if you'd let me come over to you. It's rough on the throat, all this shouting."

"You can talk from there."

"Okay. Why are you doing this? You're young, pretty. The world's full of..."

"... lies. Full of lies and flies and shit. Lies on the eyes of the dead stinking world."

"It has its good times, doesn't it?"

"I'm going to die." She spoke without emphasis, stating a fact.

"Why do you talk like that?"

"My business."

"Mine too."

She stared at him blankly for a while, and then gave a convulsive shudder. She put up a hand and drew her fingers slowly over her own face, feeling brow, cheek and mouth. She frowned.

"I don't know you."

"Name's Per Lockval."

"What?"

"Scandinavian. My father was in the whaling fleet."

Her eyes wandered away from him, came back. "Umh?"

"I said, my father was a harpoonist on a whaler."

"But you're a policeman."

"Yes." Lockval was startled. He waited for her reaction, expecting resentment, fear or maybe contempt, but the girl leaned towards him with a grave, almost wistful expression.

"There was a policeman..."

"Yes?"

"A policeman." Again, the uncertain frown crossed her face. "It was ... out east ... I think. He picked me up. He said I was all right now. Do you remember that?"

"A long time ago?"

"Umh?"

"Was it a long time ago?"

But the girl was no longer looking at him. She was edging along to her right, craning forward across the rail, and her face blazed with intense excitement.

"Who's that? Is it him, has he come?" She shook the rail with both hands. "Tell me!"

Lockval turned his head. A thin man in a sheepskin jacket moved along the gallery and appeared in the doorway. He stood with his face a little averted, so that the light from indoors touched his profile.

The girl watched him. The excitement slowly died in her. She neither moved nor spoke, but her stillness frightened Lockval as her rage had not done. He said fiercely to the newcomer, "Get out of here!"

The man stepped quickly back. Lockval said urgently,

"It's all right. He won't touch you."
"I'll never go back there."
"Sure you won't."
"He can't make me."
"That's right. Don't worry. I'm a policeman, aren't I? People have to do what I say."
Her chin lifted. "What I say."
"Okay. What you say. Whatever you say, goes."

18

TREVOR MASSIE, THE Head Accountant, was already in his office when Miss Dykes reached it at seven-fifty. With Deryk Booth, he was sorting through a bundle of cheques passed that afternoon.

He looked up as Marion came in, and his sharp little whippet's face was apprehensive.

"Is she still alive?"

"Yes. Have you found anything?"

"This, I think." He extended a cheque, filled out in a fine, pointed hand. The amount was one thousand and twenty-five, the signatory Ella Rannault. Miss Dykes nodded.

"That's the price of the fur. I have something else that may be useful. There was a buyer this afternoon, using an employee's card, who made several purchases, sent them down to Gift-Wrappings, and then failed to collect."

"The card number?"

"72.193."

Massie went to a steel cabinet and unlocked it. Inside were rows of narrow drawers, each neatly labelled with index-numbers. He pulled one forward, searched through it, extracted a card and brought it back to the desk. "Miss Ella Rannault. Address 201, Franz Place, Whytewych Dock. Employed as a temporary assistant in the Art Department." He studied the reverse side of the card. "She's done two other stints for us, 1971 and 1972. So she qualifies for store discount. We'd better check with the Art people."

"She's probably on the Advertising side."

"Well, Soper will be able to tell us. I'll give him a ring straight away. I can suggest I'm merely checking some irregularity in the card."

Booth said, "The police must have this address at once. They'll be able to send someone down to Whytewych, find out if the girl has relations or friends who can identify her, and talk sense into her."

His voice in the stuffy and overheated office had a curiously dead tone. Looking at him, Miss Dykes saw that his face was unusually pale. She said, almost on impulse, "You don't know the name, do you Deryk?"

"No, I'm afraid not."

Miss Dykes continued to watch him. She knew him so well. Everything he did was designed to serve his own interests. She had seen this sort of tension in him before and it meant he was up to something. She turned to Massie. "Does the name mean anything to you?"

"There was a boy of that name in my class at school."

"That hardly helps us. There's something ... I don't know ... familiar about her. Her face is very distinctive. Unusual. Despite her foul language, she's well-educated. And she has money. It may be easy enough to trace her family. I agree, Deryk, the police should be told at once."

Booth went away. Massie said to Marion, "Who's on the switchboard?"

"An engineer. O'Malley. Very reliable."

Soper, head of the Arts and Advertising section, knew of Ella Rannault, but could add little to the description of her, except that she was a first-rate artist. She had established a reputation as a painter and had no need to stoop to commercial art. In Soper's view, she took on the Christmas job at Kuper's because she was lonely. Very quiet, kept to herself, made no friends. Keys? God, no, nobody else in the Department had a set of keys, and Soper's were right there in his pocket. What? Certainly he would keep his mouth shut. Certainly he would be home if Massie needed him again. What the hell was going on down there?

Massie hung up at that point. He picked up the credit card from his desk and studied it.

"Throwing the tom about, wasn't she? We who are about to die blow our last cent. Does Arnold know, yet?"

"Deryk 'phoned him earlier, but he was asleep. They'll tell him when he wakes. I'll probably 'phone again soon."

"Why not leave it to Deryk? It won't help to burden Arnold with this."

Miss Dykes shook her head. Massie was a kind friend, and a marvellous accountant, but he had no understanding of human emotions. He knew little of the petty rivalries on the Board. He didn't begin to grasp the endless scheming that took place, the way little factions developed that could disrupt the whole firm if they were allowed to flourish. He was unaware of Booth's jealousy of Arnold Kuper, of his relentless ambition. Booth was capable of leaving Arnold in the dark about this suicidal girl, simply so that, later on, he could imply that Arnold was guilty of lack of concern.

Moreover, Massie had not seen the collection of gifts on the shelves downstairs, the strange assortment of gifts each bearing the single label, 'David'.

Miss Dykes, deeply troubled, left Massie to telephone the Manager of the West and Central Bank, on which Ella Rannault's cheque was drawn.

She herself went to a deserted office at the other end of the eleventh floor, and put through a call to Deirdre Kuper.

19

AS DR LUCAS moved back from the balcony, Milner said, "What's wrong, sir?"

"I'm afraid she recognised me."

"Hell, did she? Do you know her?"

"I don't remember her face. But I may have seen her at one of my clinics, possibly even when she was a child."

"You don't think she's from the Werner?"

The Werner Sanitorium was the big hospital for the mentally ill that stood on the outskirts of the city.

"If so, she was never my patient," said Lucas. "But that doesn't mean she couldn't have seen me at the hospital." As he spoke, Deryk Booth came hurrying up the staircase. He came over to Lucas and caught him by the arm

"Why don't you get out there and talk to the girl?"

"I did go out, Mr Booth. I'm afraid she knew my face."

"So?"

"She's afraid of me. Seeing me will do her more harm than good."

"Well, then, get someone else."

"I intend to try, but as I said, psychiatrists are in short supply."

"For God's sake, man, bring one in from somewhere else. Fly him up from the coast if necessary, the company will pay."

"Mr Booth," Lucas spoke sharply, and Booth's head jerked back, "panic won't help matters. I shall try and get you another doctor. In the meantime, there are several things I can do to help. I have been listening to the girl, and I've heard enough to confirm that she is seriously ill. My advice is that you leave Sergeant Lockval to talk to her. He's doing very well indeed. She appears to trust the police and fear doctors, in itself an interesting fact. I shall check the local hospitals and clinics to see if she has been treated in this town. Do you know her name?"

"Rannault," said Booth. Some of the angry colour faded from his cheeks. "Ella Rannault. She's worked on a temporary basis, over rush periods, for the past three years. She's an artist, apparently, lives in Franz Place down by the Whytewych Dock. That ring any bells?"

"Not immediately. Have you informed Police Headquarters?"

"Yes. They said they'd check their records in case she's tried this before. They'll also send someone to her home to find out what they can." Booth ran a hand over his neck. "Oh, and it seems she was shopping in the store this afternoon, and cashed a Western and Central cheque. Our Head Accountant is trying to get hold of the bank manager."

"You'll let us know what develops, sir?" said Milner.

"Of course."

"Do you know if she's married?" asked Lucas, and Milner answered, "She's not wearing any rings."

Elaine Bondi had moved gradually closer to the group, and now spoke. "It's an East Coast name, Rannault."

"Textiles," said Booth brusquely.

"No, that's not the one I mean. I've heard Sam speak about..."

Booth was staring at her, chin on chest. She met his gaze for a moment, and then sighed. "It's no use. I've forgotten."

Milner had turned towards the balcony. Keeping out of sight, he spoke in a low voice.

"Lockval?"

Lockval leaned his head back slightly.

"The name is Ella Rannault. R-a-n-n-a-u-l-t."

"Thanks."

"The doc's checking the hospitals. We'll keep you posted."

Lockval nodded. He glanced at the Spanfexa clock. He felt he'd been sitting here for a thousand years, but in fact the time was only ten minutes to eight.

20

Down on Whytewych Dock, the wind blew with increasing sharpness, plucking at the three dredgers moored there, and at the two men who now moved from their shadow onto the open wharf. The police-boat which had brought them across the river pulled back from the stone steps and moved upstream to the shelter of the yacht mole.

The plain-clothes men walked quietly past piles of timber, and crates covered with tarpaulins. A railway engine broke into stuttering motion behind them, and they waited for it to pass. The taller of the two, a man called Tarboten, whose photograph appeared regularly in *Football News*, stared at the driver and stoker.

"These buggers get more than we do."

His partner, Quincey, made no answer, but picked his way across the rails and headed for the dockyard gate. Quincey was a man of thirty-four, short, muscular, with the muddy complexion and eyeballs that showed colour somewhere in his ancestry. A lot of people made the mistake of thinking Quincey had no ambition. The fact was that he had at the age of fifteen set his targets. He wanted to be a policeman, but he did not wish to be a member of the Security Force. He wanted to own a police house in the Lombardy suburb, and a Peugeot saloon. He wanted his son to be a doctor of medicine.

All but the last of these objectives were already achieved, and Quincey had not the smallest doubt that when the time came, Dennis would enrol at the medical school at Lafitte. Quincey's aim right now was to get out of the wind blowing across Whytewych, and he didn't see any point in talking about it.

The two showed their police cards at the dockyard gate and emerged into Hogg Lane, which curved eastwards round the yacht basin. They passed the Club, a single-storey building blazing with lights, and the long row of garages and yacht-sheds behind it. Both of them knew this area well, and Quincey had been born a couple of miles down river, in the days when Whytewych was a slum. Just after the war, some developer realised that this stretch of the Old Town, built by the early merchant settlers from Holland, was worth money. The dockside stews were cleared, the stretch of houses from Hogg Lane up the hill to Franz Place being restored and sold to private ownership at a comfortable profit.

Franz Place had been the market square once, and the tall old houses made of small red bricks, with their bay windows and steep roofs, had a solid dignity still. But looking at them, Quincey decided the jet set wasn't going to move in. The lanes on the hill were so narrow they were closed to motor-traffic. No room for the Porsche here, a tycoon would have to park it down by the docks, okay in summer but no good on a night like this. All the same, the area had gone up. It was easy to see there was money on the parish register, now.

As they started round the square, a man ran past them, a big black wearing a dark tracksuit and carrying a furled umbrella. Quincey, thinking this an odd combination, peered at the runner's face and thought he had seen him before, somewhere.

"What number is it?" said Tarboten.

"This one." Quincey led the way up worn stone steps that climbed to a little terrace laid out in patterns of burned brick. There was a terracotta dog curled up on the left of the front door, and someone had tucked the evening paper under its muzzle.

Tarboten touched the pottery with his toe. "Looks real, eh?" He rang the doorbell, tilting back his head to scan the façade. "No lights, no name plate. You know how many people live here?"

"No. Most of these places have been divided into flats, but some have just the one owner."

They waited, listening to the silence in the house, hoping this wouldn't have to be one of the times they went round asking the neighbours. After a while they heard footsteps approaching from the back of the house, and a voice muttering complaints.

A chain rattled over, and the door opened a couple of inches. An old yellow face peered at them. Quincey saw black eyes veiled by lids as thin as rice-paper, a little pinched, tremulous mouth, tremulous with anger, not fear.

"Well?"

"Police, ma'am." Quincey produced his police card and held it out. She glanced at it briefly.

"So?"

"Does a Miss Ella Rannault live here?"

The old woman clicked her teeth at him. She stood in the lighted hallway and watched them, one sallow hand running up and down the edge of the door. Tarboten leaned a wrist on the jamb and smiled at her. "Come on, Gran, it's cold out here. Does Miss Rannault own this house?"

"What business of yours? Nosey cops, come round here all hours of the night. People should be having their suppers now, a bit of peace. Ask, ask, is all you think of. You don't do nothing for anyone."

"Now listen," began Tarboten, and Quincey interrupted him from the shadows. "This Miss Rannault. She's standing on a ledge ten floors up at Kuper's Stores. She says she's gonna jump."

The beaky mouth opened in shock and trembled shut again. She shook her head.

"Lyin'."

"No, it's true, Gran."

"So if it's true? What business of mine? Tonight she jumps, or maybe she doesn't. Some time it can happen."

"You think she's the suicidal type?"

"How do I know what's suicidal? I don't know what's suicidal. I can see when a woman's goin' crazy, that I can see, but suicidal is for doctors and coppers to say."

"See, now, I thought you might help to stop her." Quincey's voice had fallen into the cadences of his youth, the singsong of the fisherfolk who had once peopled this part of town. "You a smart old lady, I can see."

"No, no." She shook a claw at him. "I don't interfere. No more. They live their own way, die in their own time, I don' wanna know."

"She's young, Gran."

"And I'm old."

"This is no bloody good," muttered Tarboten, and swore as Quincey's boot caught him in the shin.

"Granma, we don't ask you to go to any trouble. Just let us come in, look around, see if she left any note, that type of thing? You do as you like, just let us go up there and take a quick look round. Umh?"

She hesitated, and then shook her head more in defeat than refusal. "Trouble. All around this house, because of her. Trouble to others. You let her go."

"Can't, Gran. My job, her trouble, see?"

The old woman sighed. She closed the door and they heard the chain fall, and they were admitted to the hall. It ran from front to back of the house, and at the far end they could see a lighted room, with a small television set and a chair draped in rugs. On their right a wooden stairway rose steeply into gloom.

"Anyone been up there today?" said Quincey.

"Not since he came down."

"Who?"

She made no answer, having already started up the stairs. Halfway up she pressed a switch and illuminated the whole well. They followed her up three turning flights, the third a short one leading back from a broad landing. A door with a Yale lock barred their way. The old woman fished a key from a pocket and unlocked the door.

Tarboten said, "Didn't tell us your name, Gran."

She spoke without looking at him. "Samuels. Mrs Zena Samuels." The door swung back and she led them into the room beyond.

It was L-shaped, the longer arm running the width of the house, the shorter extending forward towards the river. There was a bay window there, and walking towards it Quincey saw tiled and slate roofs jostling down to the water, pricked with lights already dimming as the storm closed in.

He stood pondering what he and Tarboten should do. They had no right to be searching this place, but the owner was the gainer if they did. He glanced about and found the telephone on a table near him, said to the old woman, "Mind if I call my boss? We're supposed to tell where we are."

"It's not my bills to pay."

Quincey dialled the Headquarters number and made his report. Finlander, he was informed, was on his way over to Kuper's. Quincey took the new number, dialled again and left a message with the store's switchboard.

As he turned back to the room, he saw Tarboten vanishing up a wooden stairway in the corner.

Quincey set about making a quick tour of the living-room. It was quite large, close-carpeted in dark brown shaggy wool. There was a lot of expensive modern furniture. Pictures everywhere, some framed on the walls, others tacked to boards or lying around loose. There was a stack of drawings on a map table. Quincey moved fast, checking the mantel, the grate, where a fire was made but not lit, looking at the tops of tables and inside the flap of an antique desk. A spinet stood near the desk. He opened that too, brushing the keys as he did so. The jangled notes lingered on the air.

Nowhere did he find any of the things that might help him; no photographs of the girl, or anyone else; no suicide note.

He searched the small kitchen and bathroom at the back, scanning shelves and cupboards. All the while, Mrs Samuels watched him, following him from room to room. Quincey did not try to question her. She knew a good deal more than she was telling. She looked like a woman who had seen a lot of strife, learned everything the hard way. Also, she was frail as a stick of ash. Get rough, and she'd crumble up entirely.

Quincey shifted to the bedroom.

Almost at once he leaned his head out and called, "Tarboten." The big man came tumbling down the stairs and Quincey beckoned him over. The old woman watched, rubbing fingertips across her mouth.

The bedroom was unkempt, the big double-bed unmade, silk sheets tangled across its foot. A couple of drawers had been left half-closed, but their contents were orderly. There was no sign of rifling.

"Left in a hurry," said Tarboten.

"Umh. Look over there." Quincey pointed at the dressing-table. It was of the sort that has a big circular mirror attached to it, and as Tarboten turned, he found this glass was obscured by whitish-green smears and broken lines. He went over and looked more closely.

"Soap?"

"Probably. Can't read anything, but there's half a letter 'E' near the bottom."

"My wife does that," said Quincey. "Leaves messages on the mirror. Cleans off easily." He came and stood beside Tarboten.

"Would she write a suicide note that way?"

"Why not? 'I can't live without you. E.' She leaves that on the glass, and goes off. He wakes up later and sees it. Cleans it off, to save scandal, and also leaves, maybe to try and stop her."

"How would he know where she'd gone?"

"She took his keys. That could mean she was going to one of the places he had keys for. He could check some of them by 'phone, but the store would be different. You can't 'phone a main city block and say 'Has a blonde just walked in?' "

Tarboten blew out his cheeks. "How could she be sure he'd see what she'd written?"

Quincey jerked a head at the bed. "He was lying right there. First thing he saw, when he opened his eyes, would be that mirror."

"The old woman could have cleaned the mirror. You saw what she's like, doesn't want any trouble."

"She said herself, 'Nobody's been up here since he left.' "

"That's right. We'd better talk to her."

Quincey nodded. "But let me do it. She doesn't like you."

"The hell with like and don't like."

"You leave it to me," insisted Quincey, and as so often happened, he got his way.

21

"RANNAULT? ELLA RANNAULT? Yes, of course I've heard of her!" Deirdre Kuper's voice was sharp with dismay, and the reaction frightened Miss Dykes far more than the bluster of Deryk Booth.

"Do you know her?"

"I've met her several times. She's a fine painter. She held a one-man exhibition in the Capital a few months ago. I wanted to buy one of her abstracts, but it had already been sold."

"What's she like as a person?"

"Marion, I'm not on close terms with her."

"But you must have formed some impressions?"

"I suppose ... clever, very turned-in, neurotic perhaps."

"Unbalanced?"

"Well, it's easy to suggest that now, when she's threatening suicide. Plenty of artists seem crazy to people outside the arts. Her early pictures were a bit weird, but she was still groping for her own style."

"Does David know her?"

The silence was so long that Marion repeated her question, and Deirdre said slowly. "They certainly met. Dave took me to the last day of the exhibition."

"It was his idea?"

"Not really. A common acquaintance invited us both."

"Did you get the impression that David knew Miss Rannault before?"

"What do you mean?"

"Miss Rannault spent this afternoon shopping in the store. She bought a lot of things, some very expensive, and had them gift-wrapped. Then she failed to collect them. Every last one is marked for someone called David."

"It's a common enough name, for Heaven's sake!"

"I'd like you to hear the items. Skis; silk sheets; a

Brouard watch; a set of papier-maché egg-dolls from Hong Kong; hand-mixed oil-paint and two brushes; moccasins; Bendick's chocolates; turquoise worry beads; a humming-top."

Again there was a lengthy pause. Marion had a clear picture of the woman at the other end of the line, her sharp features set, her sharp mind already calculating the threat involved. The answer, when it came, was guarded.

"It could be Dave."

"The humming-top for instance. No one could know about that unless..."

"... she knew Dave very well indeed. Do you suggest she's his mistress?"

"Deirdre, please understand, I'm not being malicious. I am just plain scared. If this girl does kill herself, there'll be an inquest. All sorts of dirt could come out of it. She could be pregnant, anything. I feel it's terribly important to find David and warn him. And there's Christine to think of, and Arnold."

"What are the police doing about it?"

"They've sent someone down to Franz Place, I think. That's where she lives."

"At Whytewych?"

"Yes, that's right."

"They may trace her family."

"What are you going to do?"

"Try and trace mine. I know some of his haunts. My advice to you, my dear, is, stay near that girl and do whatever you can to help her. Don't discuss David with anyone at all. And keep me posted every half hour or so."

"I'll do that."

"Thank you. Goodbye, Marion."

Deirdre Kuper hung up. She stood for a moment frowning at the bowl of Christmas roses on the table. Then she walked through the house to the hallway connecting with the garage; pulled a motor-coat from a closet; let herself out of the door and slipped quietly through the garage to the rear driveway.

22

AT NINE MINUTES past eight, Ella Rannault's leather bag fell from the ledge to the street below. Lockval saw her move along the ledge, saw her foot tangle in the strap, and shouted to her to watch out, but the damage was already done. The bag shot sideways, balanced for a moment on the edge, and then vanished. The girl leaned out and watched it for an instant, and then turned back. Her movements had become slower, her face more pinched, as the cold of the night bit deeper.

"Come inside now," said Lockval. "Please."

"I can't. I have very important things to do. I have to wait here."

"Wait inside, in the warm."

"He might miss me."

"Who?"

"He won't let me down."

"Please come inside."

"No! You just want to cheat me. You want to let that one take me away."

"Take it easy. I'm your friend. If you want to stay, that's all right. We'll just keep talking, umh? Anything you like is okay."

The bag burst when it hit the sidewalk.

It split wide open and spewed its contents into the gutter and under the wheels of passing traffic, a few yards from where the police car was parked.

The driver, hearing the thump of impact, climbed out and snatched up such articles as he could reach. He was stuffing them back into the bag when someone grabbed his arm.

"Officer! There's a person in that building throwing things. I could have been killed!" The woman was obese, her broad face scarlet with rage. "Look at this. Missed me by a hairsbreadth. It's a disgrace."

On the flat of her hand lay a shattered powder-compact.

The driver took it from her, opened the car door and quietly slipped the bag onto the front seat. Turning, he put a hand on the fat woman's shoulder.

"A disgrace it is, ma'am. Some typist, no doubt, at one of the windows. People are downright careless."

The woman craned her neck. "I don't see anyone at any window."

"Well you wouldn't, perhaps. Could have ducked out of sight, couldn't she, when she saw what happened?"

"So what are you going to do about it? Aren't you going to go up there and tell whoever it is they nearly killed me?"

"Can't leave the patrol car."

"I must say! I do think, after all we pay in tax ..." The woman broke off abruptly and pounced at the gutter. She came up clutching a cheque book in a letter cover. "How about that?" She pressed her nose to the window of the car. "There's a handbag in there. Someone dropped a handbag and you just put it in there this minute. I saw you. There could be money in that bag, what do you mean trying to hide it away like that?"

"I'm a policeman, lady. It's quite safe." He extended his hand. "Now, if I could have that folder?"

"I think I ought to return it to the owner."

"Madam, you can't stand here arguing. You're blocking the pavement."

"And your car's blocking the traffic. Just because you're police you think you can break any regulations you choose. I couldn't park my car here, could I?"

The woman's rising tones had already drawn a small crowd. They peered at the façade of Kuper's. A man at the back suddenly yelled, "There's someone on the ledge, up there."

Heads tilted. The man pointed an arm. "Up there. See? In that big square of light?"

The police driver tried briskness. "No one there, sir. You folks are obstructing traffic. Move on, now please. Hurry it up, will you?"

He might have saved his breath. Magically, the crowd thickened. He climbed back into the car and unhitched the radio hand-set.

Captain Finlander, called to the radio control room at Central Headquarters, asked at once what name was in the cheque book.

"E. Rannault, sir."

Finlander swore softly, then said, "Where's your mate?"

"Over the road, outside the store, main entrance."

"Call him back. I'll send up extra men. We'll have to close off Manning Lane at once, both ends, and the entrance to the underground. There'll be at least one more train stopping there, though, before the Railways can warn their drivers to carry straight on. Any passengers who do alight must be asked to use the emergency exits on the south side of the warehouse. I don't want crowds near that store. There'll be late shoppers and workers, I know, but clear them out as fast as you can. If the girl jumps, she'll hit the ground like a bomb. She'll kill anyone she lands on. You're to stay in the car from now on, Morrison, and I want reports of any developments. If I'm not here, Bushe can handle them. Finally, the girl's name is not to be released under any circumstances."

"Has she a record, sir?"

"No, but there are Rannaults in the social register. She could be news, and that I don't need."

The police measures were applied quickly and efficiently. Manning Lane was sealed off. Even so, twenty minutes after the bag landed in the roadway, there were still something like a thousand people in the immediate vicinity, and these soon became aware of the girl on the ledge.

By eight-twenty, some well-meaning person had called the Fire Brigade. Several others, intent on private gain, had placed information with newspapers, the Radio Station, and Television House.

When Captain Finlander reached Kuper's at eight-twenty-five, the incident was already in the process of becoming headlines.

23

THE MAN IN the doorway wore a dark red caftan. His hair, frizzy African hair with a reddish hue, was combed high, framing his face and neck like the ruff of a cockatoo. When he saw Deirdre Kuper he broke into a wide smile and extended long delicate hands in welcome.

"Dee my darling. I read your new book in one sitting. Come in and I will sing praises."

"I can't stay, Acky."

"My God," he was drawing her through the door, "you are quite blue with cold."

"I walked round."

He started to say something and then, catching sight of her face, merely drew her towards the fire.

"Drink?"

"No." Once inside, Deirdre seemed unable to think of anything to say, and stood contemplating a series of woodcuts laid on the divan.

"Those are nice."

"And quite irrelevant. What's on your mind?"

"David. He's gone missing at rather an important moment."

"Ah?"

"Don't be tactful, Acky, there's no time. Do you know who his latest is?"

Acqbal blinked long golden eyes. He was a man who, as the best art-dealer on the east coast, was used to fending off awkward questions, but he liked Deirdre, and trusted her. He said, "I haven't heard anything, Dee."

"Do you know Ella Rannault?"

"Yes. I've made some sales for her."

"At the moment she's threatening to jump off a tenth storey balcony at the store."

"You think, because of David?"

"It's possible. I was wondering if you could tell me ... whether in fact they knew each other well?"

"As I've said ..." he shook his head. After a moment he added, "Why don't you ask Paul November?"

"What?" She spun round to stare at him.

"Paul knows Ella very well. He's helped her a great deal, really he was responsible for her private showing."

"I didn't know he was back in town."

"Oh yes. Not to live. He just visits. But he has a lot of friends here. A lot of friends everywhere."

Deirdre seemed to be trying to collect her thoughts. She came towards Acqbal. "Could you get hold of November for me?"

"I'll try."

"Now!"

"Certainly." He crossed the room, searched for a number in the index beside the telephone, dialled. Over his shoulder he said, "He has a pad near the river, but he's seldom in." They listened to the steady burr, burr sound. Acqbal shrugged. "No answer."

"Could you keep trying, Acky? And if you get him, tell him to 'phone me. Don't say why. Do that for me."

"Of course. I have an empty evening looming. I'll sit on the 'phone." He leaned down and wrote on the desk pad.

"This is his number, and the address, if you want to try and get him yourself."

"Thanks. But my problem is I have to leave our line free. Calls are coming through from the store."

"Don't worry." He was following her to the door. "I'll chase November, and in between whiles I'll chase Dave."

"Bless you."

As Deirdre walked back along the street, little traffic passed. The wind blew strongly, gusting through every open space. She thought that in a couple of hours it would snow.

24

CHRISTINE WAS IN the television room at the back of the house. It was a comfortable room, furnished with heavy rugs and curtains from Lesotho peasant looms. Marvellous heat flowed from the tiled hearth. The TV set in the corner was switched on and Christine sat on the floor in front of it. On screen, a woman was demonstrating how to make Christmas candles.

Deirdre came and stood by the fire. "Has anything come over?"

"No. Where have you been?"

"I walked down to Acky's. I thought he might know where Dave is." She began to pull off her car-coat, her movements lethargic as if she struggled in some invisible snowdrift. "Do you think Dave is holed-up somewhere?"

"Why should he be?"

"I don't know. If he's done something worse than usual ... or if there's a a problem he can't handle ... he might rat."

Christine shrugged, her eyes still on the television picture.

"A while ago," said Deirdre, "you mentioned a take-over bid."

"That was nothing. Just rumours."

"I see." Deirdre suddenly seemed to recover strength. "That girl at the store, they know her name. It's Rannault. Ella Rannault."

Christine turned her head. "Did Acky say so?"

"No. Marion 'phoned, before I went out. The girl bought a lot of presents in the store this afternoon. They identified her through her credit-card. Does the name mean anything to you?"

"No."

"You're sure, Chris?"

"I've never heard of her."

Deirdre moved across to the window-seat and twitched aside the curtain. The night was settling like a cat to a meal, hunching yellow shoulders. She let the curtain fall again.

"Marion says that everything the girl bought was gift-wrapped for someone called 'Dave'. She thinks it might be our David."

"Why? Why should she think that?"

"They were the sort of things he likes."

"Such as?"

"A humming-top. A set of Chinese dolls."

"Toys?" Christine sounded incredulous. "Are you trying to tell me Dave has children with this woman?"

"No. But those items are rather ... disturbing. Come over and sit here and I'll explain."

As the young woman unwillingly took a place on the window-seat, Deirdre seemed to be marshalling her thoughts. At last she said, "There were a good many presents. Skis, a Brouard watch, moccasins. All things Dave said he wanted for Christmas. But the toys, as you call them, are another matter. They relate to the past. They recall a time in David's life ... in my life ... that I thought was forgotten. When he was a child he owned a top called Singsong, and a set of those egg-dolls. Has he ever mentioned them to you?"

"No."

"And yet, it seems, this Miss Rannault knew of them?"

There was a short silence. Christine sat with downcast eyes, one finger tracing the pattern of the cushions. "All right. All right, so she knew him well. Maybe they've been having an affair. It looks as if it's over, doesn't it, since she's ready to jump off the roof? He'll come skipping back, soon enough."

"I wouldn't count on it."

"What's that supposed to mean?"

"Chris, please don't lose your temper with me. We're headed for a crisis, all of us, and if we can't work things out quietly ... Please just listen to what I say. I know Ella Rannault, very slightly. She's an artist. She has a studio down on Whytewych Dock, quite close to the

Yacht Club. Dave uses the Club a lot."

"Okay," Christine gave her triangular smile. "So he has the opportunity."

"And the motive."

"A nut-case painter?"

"No. The painting world. He belonged to it once. I think he's gone back to it."

"You say that as if he was back on the Big H."

"He could be. Art is a drug. You wouldn't understand."

"I understand he's not hooked on painting. He hasn't touched a brush for years. He told me himself, if he couldn't be in the top bracket, he wasn't going to dabble. I know Dave. He likes success, and he likes money. I think he did the right thing when he joined Kuper's. He's doing what he wants to do."

"Until tonight, I'd have agreed with you. Now, I don't know." Deirdre took an enamelled cigarette case from her pocket, opened it on the window-ledge and pushed it towards Christine. She herself took a cigarette and sat turning it in her fingers. "When I spoke to Acky tonight, he told me that a man named Paul November is a great friend of this Ella Rannault. You've heard of him, I take it?"

"Something."

"He's a sculptor. He's very controversial, but he's also recognised as a great. We used to know Paul, a long time ago before he got famous."

Deirdre laid the unlit cigarette aside and ran both her hands upwards through her hair. She sat like that, holding her temples and staring at Christine. "When Dave had the humming-top and the egg-dolls. That long ago. And now he's back. I don't know how he affects us, but I'm dead sure he does. I think something is happening that none of us understands, something that goes to the root of things."

Christine watched her without speaking.

"I feel," continued Deirdre, "that this woman may be someone much more ... significant ... in Dave's life, than anyone that's happened before. Than you, Chris, or any of his other women. I'm not saying this to hurt you. I'm not even talking about love. 'Significance' is the only word to describe what I mean. She has come close to the centre of his life. Do you believe that there is this central point in each of us? That there are some things that lie deep, deep in a person's being and are sacrosanct?"

"Yes."

"And if you injure someone at this vital point, then it's an injury that can never be repaired?"

Christine nodded.

"I'm terribly afraid," said Deirdre, "that we injured David in that way. Arnold and I. He may not have forgiven us. He may have been waiting, all this long time, perhaps without knowing it, for some sort of revenge. Now this woman Ella Rannault, and Paul November, coming into his life together, have given him his chance."

There was silence in the room, except for the small muttering made by the flames in the grate. Christine's bravado suddenly fell away. She began to tremble and sat with her arms folded across her breast.

"He didn't come home last night," she said. "I lied. We had an argument at dinner. He walked out and he hasn't been back. Oh Jesus, Dee, help me, I'm so frightened."

25

CAPTAIN FINLANDER ARRIVED at Manning Lane at 8.25. The police car that brought him dropped him at the east end of the street, where it joined Porter's Way. There was already a sizeable crowd pressing against the two vans that had been drawn across the intersection. Faces craned towards Finlander, voices shouted questions.

Finlander ignored them, ducked between the vans and spoke to the Sergeant in charge.

"Is she still okay?"

"Yes, sir." The Sergeant tilted his head far back. "It's just on two hours now. She must be fair numb."

"Any Press yet?"

"No."

"Just a matter of time. It came over the 8.30 news flash that she was up there. Someone must have 'phoned 'em. Who's on the other end of the Lane?"

"Noyce."

"And these buildings?" Finlander indicated the towering face of the warehouses on the south side.

"Cleared."

"The Station?"

"Closed. We got as many people away as we could before the news broke. There'll be more coming this way, now."

"Well, keep 'em back." Finlander glanced along the Lane. On both sides, there were still a number of lighted windows, some in Kuper's itself, some in the Mission building. People clustered there, staring upwards. Ringside view.

It was nothing new to him, this morbid curiosity of the masses. It was a problem on its own. The girl might jump or she might not, that was something for Lockval to worry about, with Milner and Dr Lucas.

His first worry had to be the audience down here. The girl was already news. In a little while she was probably going to be on the national circuits. For a few hours, or maybe minutes, she was going to fix the interest of millions of goofers across the country, and a lot of them were going to exert influence of one kind or another. Thousands might come down here, try and shove past the police blocks to get a closer view of death. Others would be a bloody nuisance in other ways. Finlander knew it all. Criticism, abuse, 'phone-calls from V.I.P.s. They would say the police shouldn't allow nuts to jump off ledges. Then there'd be the people who sold blood by the litre. Reporters, from the papers and television, all in the public interest, with plenty of sour things to say if you didn't let 'em in close.

Finlander checked the whole street himself. He had already spent time on the 'phone, speaking to the owner of every property on the block, asking them to keep their doors locked, warning them to deny access to anyone not holding a police card or an official pass. The railway police were looking after the area behind the warehouses. A lot of men pulled off routine duty, simply because one suicidal nut meant crowds, and crowds meant traffic snarls, and pick-pockets, and drunks, and car-nabbing, and trouble for policemen.

Back in the middle of the street, he stared up the dizzy canyon. He picked out the square of light that marked the tenth-floor balcony. He saw the spidery dark figure on the ledge.

The driver of the police car climbed out and saluted. "Sir? Would a bit more light help? There's a couple of Army trucks parked in the Mission yard. One of the men came and told me they've got a portable spotlight. Maybe a warehouse could supply the power."

Finlander smiled. "Thanks Morrison, but I think it's better as it is. If we shine a spot on her, she may panic and peel off. I'm going in now. It may be, as time goes on, there'll be people I want passed through. I'll let you know and you can relay it to the men at each end of the Lane."

"Right, sir."

Finlander walked towards Kuper's. The display windows were still lit. He looked past kitchen-ware and crockery to the centre of the main hall. There was a sort of glass tank there, with an illuminated sign above it, 'Gift-Wrappings'. A man with a guard dog was patrolling the area. He caught sight of Finlander and raised a hand in greeting. Finlander sketched an answer. A lot of security men were ex-policemen.

At the main entrance, a uniformed man stepped from the shadows and came to meet him, holding out a parcel.

"Miss Rannault's bag, sir."

"Is everything back inside it?"

"Yes."

"Remember, her name is not to be released unless and until I give permission."

The constable looked an enquiry. Finlander said, "There's a Rannault in Eastern Coasters, and another in Federal Banks."

"Jesus."

"Umh."

"Does the Press know she's up there, sir?"

"Yes."

Finlander was about to go through the door when a voice hailed him from across the street.

"Officer? Excuse me, Officer?"

Finlander checked impatiently. Three people were hurrying towards him; a soldier, a man in a fur hat, and a clergyman. The last crossed the pavement and said, "I'm sorry to delay you, Captain."

"Well?"

"My name is Teale, I'm from the Mission. I have an offer of help."

Finlander hesitated. A padre might be able to talk to the kid. On the other hand, she might have a hate on religion. The little preacher, however, was shaking his head.

"Oh, I don't mean myself. I've no experience of this sort of thing, and I imagine you have. It's Sergeant Coggin here who has the proposition. He's attached to the Fifth Mountain Corps, and he and Mr Smail were discussing the fact that there's no way to reach the girl, except from the balcony. Henry, I think you should speak for yourself."

The soldier stepped forward into the light. He said, "It's just, maybe we could get a net across the street. I'd need a closer look at the set-up, of course."

Finlander sighed. "A net? Ten stories up?"

"I've worked a lot higher." Coggin screwed up his eyes, measuring. "And wider. Maybe not so handsome."

"While you were slinging your net, she'd be on her way down. She's a nut-case. These suicides, you don't know what will trigger 'em off. The idea is always there inside, see? You make a wrong move, say the wrong word, that girl will jump. I can't take chances. Thanks for the try, though."

The soldier shrugged and began to turn away, but the second civilian blocked him and leaned towards Finlander.

"Captain, my name is Smail. I work here. I've been telling the Sergeant, I know this building better than my own house. I know that balcony. The overhang is considerable, and there are big windows on the ninth floor, directly beneath. You could work without being seen by the young woman. I do beg of you to consider it."

Finlander frowned. "I know your face."

"Yes. The shop-lifting last year."

"Oh yes." Finlander gave his bleak smile and turned back to Coggin. "Well, the Fire Department have sent a couple of men over. You could talk to them. Come in, all of you."

The three men entered the store. The doors were closed again, the constable took up his post.

At the west end of Manning Lane a slight disturbance was taking place. A very tall man, a black, was trying to persuade a policeman to allow him past the barrier. Asked to give his name, and the reason for his anxiety to reach Kuper's, he clammed up. After a while he seemed to come to a decision, for he moved rapidly away down the block. Constable Noyce, who had him marked down as a trouble-maker, watched him until he turned down the lane that led to Parade Square. There was always the chance that he'd gone off to collect reinforcements. But he never reappeared, and Noyce, having plenty more urgent things on his mind, soon forgot all about him.

26

THE RECEPTIONIST AT the Parade Square Hotel was immune to sartorial anomalies, so when a black man in a track-suit, carrying a rolled umbrella, came up to his desk, he merely said "Good evening, sir", in a pleasant voice.

"Evening." The black man smiled briefly. "Could I borrow your East Coast telephone book, please?"

"Certainly." The clerk slid the directory across the counter. "You want to book a long-distance call?"

"Is that possible? I'm not a resident."

"No matter. You're Paul November, aren't you?"

"Yes."

"Recognised you from your picture in *Connoisseur*."

"You're observant." The black man found the number he wanted, jotted it down on a desk pad and pushed it over.

"Won't get much of a reception in this weather," said the clerk. He studied the electric clock overhead. "Eight-forty. If you care to wait another twenty minutes, you'd get the call on cheap rates."

"This can't wait," said Mr November.

27

"IT WASN'T PAUL'S fault," said Deirdre. "He never for one moment suspected he could cause us harm, or he'd have cleared out of the district. He had that sort of drastic simplicity. Perhaps it's the nature of his genius."

If Christine heard her, she gave no sign. She leaned back in the shadows with the blank expression of a child whose mind, unbeguiled by some comforting tale, scurries in secret tunnels of its own.

"When I first met Paul," continued Deirdre, "he was about eighteen years old, working as a quarry-blaster, because that gave him the chance to buy cheap stone. Later, he moved about a good deal, served an apprenticeship with a stone-mason, studied art and anatomy. Whenever he ran out of funds, he'd come back to the quarry and take a job there for a few months.

"He was interested only in sculpture. His technique was still clumsy, but whatever he produced had great force.

He seemed able to release the power buried in the rock, and he had the same gift with people. He was one of the first people to encourage me to write. He understood that I was unhappy, before I realised it myself. He tried to help, when no one else gave a damn."

Deirdre's face had become rapt. She moved restlessly on the window-bench, and her hair tossed about her face and the firelight shone on her dark clothes and pale flickering hands.

"All these years, I've never spoken to anyone. I've let people think what they like. I know what they've said about the way Arnold and I live. I'm supposed to be an alcoholic, aren't I, a nympho, anything that will put a bit of spice into their mediocre lives? I won't fight their gossip, it's beneath contempt, but I realise my silence has been unfair to you. You deserve an explanation.

"We never had a very good marriage, Arnold and I. We were ill-suited. Our backgrounds were too different. My father was a scholar and an agnostic. He taught me that the one vice was hypocrisy, and the one virtue the dispelling of illusion. I grew up believing that once you knew the truth, everything else was irrelevant.

"Then I married Arnold and came into quite a different world. There, compromise was the chief virtue. You had to meet the other man's price, you had to cut corners, you had to give and take. I couldn't learn the trick of Arnold's world, any more than he could be happy in mine. He spoke of the truth as 'cruelty'. He read my books and found them cruel. He said I 'went too far'. I didn't think it was possible to go too far in analysis, but that was the phrase he used to sum me up. I went too far.

"Life in town just emphasised our difficulties. There was a circle of people I disliked and who disliked me. It seemed to me that they went much farther than I did, sometimes right over the brink of honesty, but this was passed off as know-how or drive. Once, when I challenged Arnold about one of his cronies, he told me that our money came from these sources, and I enjoyed it, therefore it was hypocritical to accept the takings and criticise the dealer. I had to agree with him.

"The saving grace in our lives was the farm. We bought it soon after we were married. It was up in the apple-belt. We didn't live there, because Arnold's father had just died, and we were building up Kuper's, but we went out there as often as we could.

"At that time, Arnold was very like Dave is now; successful and dissatisfied at the same time, feeling there wasn't enough to fill his life and yet not sure what else he wanted. He was interested in politics. It was the time of the depression, and there was talk of the need for labour reform. There was poverty everywhere. Even pulling through a rich farm like ours was a challenge. Arnold worked the land properly, he didn't run it at a loss for tax purposes. He identified himself with life in the country, and with countrymen. We had black and white labour. Most of the skilled work was done by whites, and the unskilled by blacks. The November family was an exception.

"Davey was born up at Crossthwaite. He loved it. He resented the time we had to spend in town. Then, when he was six, he contracted meningitis. He nearly died and after his recovery he was delicate for a long time. That was when Arnold suggested we make the farm our permanent home. I admit I jumped at the chance.

"We moved lock, stock and barrel. We already had plenty of friends on the neighbouring farms and in the village. Paul's father was a clerk in the store, and his mother had been a teacher. The quarry where Paul worked was on the edge of our land and he used to cross the fields rather than go round by the road. He often stopped to chat.

"Crossthwaite is a beautiful place, high enough in the hills to give it a marvellous climate. The winters were hard sometimes, but the rains were gentle, we could grow things like peonies and lily of the valley. Out there, Arnold and I became a little more like each other. I compromised, and Arnold dropped some of his pretences.

"We had three good years. The village school was a good one and David enjoyed going there, but he'd missed a lot through illness, and so we asked Mrs November to give him extra lessons at home. She was a big strapping woman with a mouthful of gold teeth. Her husband was small and gentle. One of his ancestors had been a slave, that's where the name 'November' came from; the month of his sale to a new owner.

"The November family saved us many times. Davey was not strong. He suffered from terrible headaches that left him weak for days, and kept him away from school. He looked forward so much to seeing Mrs November. She always brought an old basket with something good in it, biscuits or smoked sausage, or toys she'd made herself. I remember a farmyard of animals all made of acorns and pins. Sometimes she'd just have a riddle or puzzle for him, or a couple of stamps. Once she brought something very precious, a set of Chinese egg-dolls that had been in her family for a long time. They were beautifully made. The ones you see now are just machine copies, but those were the work of a craftsman and David treasured them. Another time, she brought a humming-top. David called it Singsong and believed it had magic properties.

"Just before his tenth birthday, I fell pregnant. Arnold and I were both very happy about it. But when the child was born, she was deformed, without arms, and she died the next day. I'm told the deformity was due to drugs I was given, although at the time the thalidomide danger wasn't known and the doctors spoke of congenital defect. I somehow felt responsible. I came out of hospital with a terrible sense of guilt and I couldn't throw it off. I must have been very hard to live with.

"Again, it was the Novembers who saved us. Paul was doing a spell at the quarry, and every day, before and after work, he'd come in to see us. David particularly needed company, as Arnold was away during the week. Paul taught him to draw, and found he had some talent. At weekends, the two of them would work together in

Paul's barn, and I could see that David was improving by leaps and bounds, not only in skill but in health as well.

"I suppose I should have foreseen that Davey might come to lean too much on Paul. It wasn't just that David was the novice and Paul the expert. It was Paul's own personality. I don't know if you've seen pictures of him, but they don't convey him. He's massively tall and broad, very dark-skinned, and his features have something Arabic, the nose thin and the eyes large and brilliant. I've often wondered if he's a descendant of the Africans who made the Ife heads. And above all, he has this animal vitality that sweeps you along.

"David and I sometimes sat and watched him work. You can't imagine the muscle and will-power and stamina it takes to subdue stone, let alone make it live again in a new form. Can you see how for David, who watched these miracles, Paul November began to be a god?

"By the end of summer, when Paul went back to the city, we were all committed to a friendship that seemed irreversible. Arnold was a little on the outside of it, but he understood that David loved Paul in the way a child loves a hero, setting him apart; and because Paul handled this love so kindly, so generously and with such tact, Arnold could only be grateful.

"Over the next two years, we saw that the hero-worship wasn't all that misplaced. There was a good deal of the heroic in Paul. He went through all the tribulations of being poor, and a black man, and came out triumphant. Above all, this larger-than-life quality showed in his work, and people who mattered could recognise it. He began to build an important reputation.

"The one subject in which he took no interest was politics. He had no colour feeling and no bitterness, and politics was for him something rather amusing, like a circus act. His parents were militantly liberal, but Paul never took any part in our discussions. Sometimes, when someone spoke of 'the colour problem', he'd grin and put his hand on his chest and say 'that's me'. He was joking, but Arnold and I began to feel that Paul was a symbol. When we thought of racial prejudice, it was prejudice against Paul; Paul excluded from the best art school in the country because all the bursaries were reserved for whites; Paul turned away from a sleazy hotel; Paul a prophet in his own country.

"When you face this sort of living reproach, you can't ignore it. You have to be changed by it in some way.

"In the year David turned twelve, the Government launched its Nicol plan. This was a land-development scheme that involved buying up the small-holdings along the River Crosse, which had been owned by coloured families for generations. The district was sharply divided about it. Some of the landowners inland felt it was necessary, because the small-holdings were uneconomic; others, like Arnold, believed it was totally wrong to shift a whole community from its roots.

"The Novembers were one of the families that would be forced to move. Marie November felt it very deeply. Her husband was a white-collar worker, but she stemmed from the land, and couldn't imagine living anywhere but at Crossthwaite. One night, when they were having supper with us, she looked at Arnold and said, with a half-smile, 'When the election comes, you must stand, Mr Kuper. We need you.'

"Arnold laughed it off, but I could see the idea had taken hold. He'd sit for long spells, thinking, and he started reading up on the policies of the Federal Party. A couple of months later, a senior member of the Party approached him and asked him to stand, and he said he'd accept nomination.

"Well, I was pretty terrified. Neither of us had any idea of how to run a campaign. There were other obstacles, too. Arnold's business partners didn't like the idea of his entering politics, they said he hadn't the time. They wouldn't have beefed about a contest in a smart urban seat, some of the kudos would have come to Kuper's, but who wanted to argue about a row of potato-patches in hick territory? The Press, however, took it up. Arnold made some speeches and statements that got good coverage and a prominent opponent was stupid enough to try smear tactics against him, which improved his chances overnight.

"Before the winter set in, Arnold was a bright new star in the electoral sky. The *Herald* did a Profile of him, describing him as the champion of the rural poor, and he had letters from right across the country, expressing support for his stand.

"But the election was still months away, and the Christmas truce came round. On Christmas Eve some of us took the school choir round, carol-singing. It was very cold, and at a lot of the farmhouses they handed out hot rum punch or wine, so by the time we got back to the village we were all pretty noisy.

"As we passed the railway-station, David suddenly shouted, 'There's Paul! Paul's back!' We all piled out and ran up into the station yard. Paul was there, standing beside a truck, and on the back of the truck was an enormous block of dark marble. Everyone crowded round, yelling and asking him whose tombstone it was going to be, and he kidded back. But when he looked at the marble his face had a shine like a full moon.

" 'What's it going to be, Paul?' I said, and he smiled at me.

" 'Immortality,' he said.

" 'Whose?'

"He stood there, smiling a little, and then he put out his big rough hands and touched the stone very gently, as if he were feeling the beat of its heart. And I knew the immortality he spoke of was something he could not define, but it was there, inside the marble, waiting for him to release it."

28

"OH, DAVEY-BOY, WHY don't you come?"

The muttering voice spoke from the balcony, and the listeners on the gallery bent closer to the doorway.

"Cold. I'm cold," said the voice. Sergeant Lockval's deep tones answered.

"Come in, lass. Maybe he's waiting for you at home."

The girl made no reply. Deryk Booth glanced up at Marion Dykes, who was nearest the door. She shook her head.

Down on the sales floor, the telephone rang sharply, and Elaine Bondi ran down to answer it. She spoke a few words, and then turned and made a beckoning signal. Booth and Marion went to join her. As they approached, Elaine framed the word "Reporter". Booth took the receiver from her hand.

"Deryk Booth speaking."

"Good evening, Mr Booth. This is Phil Hackett of Cross-Country Television. We've received a report that a woman is threatening a suicide leap from the tenth floor of Kuper's. Can you confirm this is so?"

"I have nothing to say to you."

"Mr Booth, with respect, that's a pretty unrealistic attitude to adopt. The police have closed Manning Lane to traffic, the Railways are diverting Underground trains, there's already a big crowd gathering in the Parade area. If there is a woman, as described, then some accurate reporting might help you. I do urge you to..."

"Nothing to say," repeated Booth, and slammed down the receiver.

Marion Dykes eyed him. "I think that's foolish. It won't stop them, you know."

Booth gave her a furious glance. "Never mind that. I know how to handle nosey-parkers. I want to know what the police think they're doing, closing the street? Don't they know that'll attract more attention than anything?"

"If she jumps," said Marion, "her body will hit the

ground with terrific force. They can't risk her falling on pedestrians, or even a motor vehicle. And I'm telling you that you can't fend off the Press and Television. It would be far better to plan what to say, and give them something definite."

"Such as?"

Marion glared back at him. She put out a hand and lifted the receiver, shifting the 'phone out of Booth's reach.

"What do you think you're doing?"

Miss Dykes turned her back and spoke to the operator.

"Mr O'Malley? The call that just came through was from Cross-Country Television. You'll probably get a lot of calls from the Press."

"Already started, Miss Dykes. There's lights all over the flamin' board."

"Calls from the police, or Mr Kuper's house, must come through to us here. Some of the smart Alecs will try to hoodwink you, but you must try to establish the identity of every caller. If it's anyone concerned with the Press or Television, tell them that it's true there's a girl on the ledge. Say the matter is being handled by the police and a psychiatrist, and that we have been warned that people must be kept away from Kuper's, for their own and the girl's safety. Say that a further bulletin will be released in due course. If you feel you can't handle any call in this way, then refer it to Mr Booth or me. Thank you."

Across the counter, her eyes challenged Booth. He said, "They'll be round your ears like hornets."

"Possibly." She was watching him closely. "I'm usually the one to plead for privacy, Deryk. You always say we must take the Press into our confidence. What's different now?"

"The circumstances, surely? We don't have a suicide every day. I'd prefer silence until we've had an opportunity to talk to a senior member of the police." He was beginning to lash himself into a self-righteous rage. "It's a disgrace that we've been left to deal with underlings. I shall have something to say..."

"Say it to the man at the top," advised Miss Dykes. Her eyes were fixed on the distant elevator foyer. "Seems you're going to be given your chance right now."

Two men moved through the archway into the salesroom. One of them was a minister of religion. The other was a captain of police, thickset, with crinkly red hair cropped short. As soon as he came up to the group by the counter, he said briskly, "Miss Dykes?"

Marion Dykes held out her hand, which was enveloped.

"I'm Captain Finlander. We spoke on the telephone. This is Mr Barry Teale of the Methodist Mission."

Teale smiled at Booth. "We've met."

Booth nodded briefly. "Indeed. This is my secretary, Mrs Bondi. Captain, I have to tell you I don't feel we are getting any protection here. We are being nuisanced by the Press. Is there no way you can protect us against this sort of pest?"

"Not really," said Finlander. "We've cordoned off the area and nobody will get in close now without an official pass, but that will include bona fide Pressmen. I doubt if you're wise to antagonise them, sir. They'll get their stories anyhow, and it'll be better for you if they don't have to pay too much for 'em."

"Pay?"

"Sure." The Captain's sandy brows expressed impatience. "There's always someone ready to peddle another man's grief."

"It's disgusting."

"Blame the people who buy newspapers. They like dirt. Did the Press appear to know the girl's name?"

"I don't think so," said Miss Dykes.

"Good. I'd like to keep it that way. You did a good job finding it out. Is the Bank Manager coming over?"

"Yes. I spoke to him myself. His name is Flory."

"Fine." Finlander turned to Booth. "I've sent two men down to the girl's home address."

"You seem to be putting about half the Force onto this affair. You think the girl is that important?"

Finlander looked Booth over without saying anything. Then he turned back to Marion Dykes.

"I'm going to try and withhold publication of the name until after the nine o'clock news; unless anything happens to change my mind. Now, if you'll excuse me, I must talk to my own men, and Dr Lucas."

Finlander walked across the sales floor and up the steps to the gallery. As he reached this, he glimpsed through the open doors the seated bulk of Lockval, and beyond that a greyish blurred face against the sky. He did not pause, but turned right and moved a short distance along the gallery. Milner and Dr Lucas followed him.

"Well, how's it?"

"Lockval's keeping her going, sir, but I don't know for how long. She won't tell us anything about herself. If you ask her too many questions, she goes wild, yells and swears and so on. But she's been quieter, the last hour."

Finlander transferred his glance to Lucas, and the little doctor nodded. "Unfortunately, she won't let me near her. She's apparently recognised me. But from what I've seen and heard, I'd say she's a schizoid type, probably manic-depressive."

"That mean she might jump?"

"Yes." Lucas hesitated. "She's almost certainly psychotic, and might kill herself. During the time I've been here, she's been sliding from a state of elation or extreme excitement to one of depression. The fact that she knew me, prompted me to check on the Werner Hospital. I know the Superintendent. He'll try and let me know if she's been a patient there, but one has to obtain certain clearances to release such information."

"She signed her cheques 'Ella Rannault'. The name mean anything to you?"

"No."

"The cheque book in her bag shows she drew two thousand this afternoon, but there was very little cash in her purse. She must have been on quite a spending spree."

"I think so. I heard the two ladies talking. Miss Dykes

and the young one. It seems the girl bought a fur coat which she's now wearing."

"Do you buy a fur coat to commit suicide?"

Lucas raised round bright eyes. "I've known a man dress up in full regimentals. But it could also mean she planned to stay warm while she staged a fake attempt."

"Why should she do that?"

"To get attention. To exert pressure on someone. She's talked of a man called Davey. She said, 'Davey, why don't you come?' I think it's likely she left a note for him somewhere."

Milner nodded. "I reckon that's the way of it, sir. Most likely this chap ditched her, and she thinks she'll scare him into coming after her."

"And if he doesn't come?"

"He'd better," said Lucas.

"Well," said Finlander, "keep at it. Milner, spell Lockval if he gets tired, but not unless it's really necessary. I have to tell you the Fire Department boys are checking over the floor directly under this one. They've got a wild man from the Mountain Corps with them, who thinks he can put a net across the street. They'll let us know soon as they can. I want to talk to this Miss Dykes. She's got something on her mind that she's not telling."

He started to move away, then turned back. "Miss Rannault's Bank Manager is coming over, doc. I'd like you to be present when he says his piece. Okay?"

"I'll be here." Lucas glanced towards the balcony. "Let's hope she will, too."

29

WHILE FINLANDER WAS up in the gallery, the Reverend Mr Barry Teale remained on the sales floor. He stood quietly beside a counter draped with silks and wondered whether he should quietly leave. There was no reason for staying. He did not flatter himself he could do anything for the girl on the ledge. He had never belonged to Lifeline, or the other organisations that dealt with would-be suicides, and he was certain in his own mind that only people with special experience should attempt such work. If there had been no one else ready to talk to her, he might have tried, but it appeared the police had the right boy for the job, and Dr Lucas was a respected psychiatrist.

Nowadays, one couldn't be sure that people in trouble wanted a priest. Mr Teale had no illusions about the rôle of the preacher in modern society. It was, most times, a walk-on part. You didn't play the lead, or even a big part, except in Christmas and Easter productions, and then you were billed for a limited season. Most church members were nominal. They didn't expect their preacher to drop in, even in times of stress. Sometimes one was pleasantly surprised. A street accident, a child lost, somebody dying, and suddenly the priest was the only man who could help. We are, thought Teale, a sort of hot-line to God, to be used only in extreme emergency.

So it would be exhibitionist and possibly downright harmful to take the stage in the present drama. One could pray for the girl's safety over at the Mission as well as here. Why stay? Because, like the police or Coggin or the store people, he had a professional interest? Was that what the girl needed, or did she need someone who cared about her, in a direct and personal way?

While Teale stood, self-effacing, uncertain, the woman who had been introduced as Miss Marion Dykes came up to him. She was plain, he saw, with a square jaw, a sallow skin, and rather small brown eyes. She had an air of great determination, and to Teale's experienced eye, of deep anxiety. He had noticed, at the time of introduction, that she had watched Mr Booth somewhat warily. The pair would seem to be old rivals. That wasn't unusual in the business world.

As she came up to him, Teale gave her his disarming smile, which produced in her that double-take reaction that meant she had been about to say something brusque.

He said, "You must be wishing me at the bottom of the sea, Miss Dykes."

She blinked, and then gave a half-smile. "No. Myself rather." She ran a tired hand over one shoulder, as if the muscles ached. "You must be uncomfortable, standing here. There's a chair."

"I'm much more comfortable than that poor girl. It must be bitterly cold for her."

"Yes. And she's frail-looking. I'm terrified that even if she doesn't intend to ... to jump, she might turn giddy, and fall."

"You think her threats are empty?" Teale picked up the chair she had indicated, and moved it towards her. Almost without thinking, she sank down into it, and Teale realised she had a desperate wish to confide in someone. She raised her eyes to his and said simply, "This is the most terrible thing that has ever happened to me. I suppose I've been lucky."

He nodded, and she said, "There is a great deal happening that I don't understand."

"It's the human condition."

"Yes. But this girl ... you asked if she's shamming. I think she is. But the doctor says she is mentally deranged, and he obviously knows his job."

"She could be both sick ... insane ... and shamming, couldn't she? The insane frequently act out very complicated parts."

Miss Dykes made no answer, and Teale said gently, "You could talk to the doctor yourself, you know."

"I'm scared."

"Why? Because he's a psychiatrist?"

"Because he might see through me. It's not the girl I care about. It's the people she may harm by her actions. I care about them." Her voice reached the brink of tears. "Mr Arnold Kuper ... the owner of this store ... is a very sick man. He has emphysema."

"Does he know what is happening?"

"I'm not sure. I telephoned his home. He had an attack

earlier this afternoon, and has been resting. His wife has promised to tell him as soon as he wakes."

"The shock will be unpleasant, no doubt; but perhaps it may not come to the point of telling him. They may talk the girl round, before then."

"No. She'll never capitulate."

"That's a strange word to use. Do you feel she's at war with us?"

"She's at war with someone. She'll die rather than give in." Miss Dykes seemed startled by her own intuitions. She looked squarely at the minister. "This afternoon, she bought a great number of articles in this shop and had them gift-wrapped for someone named David. I have reason to suppose they were meant for someone I know. David Kuper, Arnold's son."

"I see."

"I don't know why I'm saying all this to you. It's none of your concern."

"It is now."

"I don't normally ... oh, Lord, the truth is that I believe there is some sordid affair between this girl and David. If she kills herself, there will be a dreadful scandal. You see?"

Teale put a hand on her shoulder. "I doubt it. Today, the world takes a deal of shocking."

"I don't worry about them. Only about Arnold. He's a very strict man, very proud."

"If, as you believe, she's shamming, then she has a motive, even a twisted one. Do you think she's trying to influence someone? David Kuper himself, for example?"

"Perhaps."

"In that case, she will have communicated with him in some way, left him a note, or a message of some sort. No doubt the police will be searching her own home for that? They do know her identity I assume?"

"Yes. Her name is Ella Rannault."

Teale's face went blank. "R-a-n-n-a-u-l-t?"

"That's right."

"I don't know her, but the surname's familiar to me. There's a huge clan of them, living mainly on the East Coast. They have interests in shipping, foodstuffs, textiles, property. One branch owns the Mission where I work. So you could say that the Rannaults are all that stands between me and the bull-dozer. It's a strange coincidence, isn't it?"

"Too damn strange," said Marion Dykes.

30

ON THE NINTH floor Mr Smail, the two men from the Fire Department, and Sergeant Coggin, considered the view from the windows.

"Look at the buggers," said one of the firemen, indicating a black clot at one end of Manning Lane. "Never miss, do they? The more bodies, the better. Kill a guy, blocking the ambulance, trampling the 'oses if you let 'em." He grunted, withdrawing his head. "Tell you flat, we'll never get the rig up 'ere."

They were standing in a stock-room. About six paces to their rear stretched shelves packed with boxes. The wall they faced was breached by four tall windows that lay directly beneath the overhang of the tenth-floor balcony. To right and left ran heavy buttresses.

The junior fireman pointed across the street. "What about the ware'ouse? Roof's flat. Big doors on the ground floor, big lifts. Might get a small rig up that way, and throw a ladder over to this side."

"An' arst the lady kindly to step over? Yer can stuff that one, chum."

Coggin was leaning his elbows on the window-ledge, his gaze on the buttress to his right. "You can't climb up, that's for sure. The overhang's too big. But you might get a net across."

"How?" said the first fireman, and Coggin stood up and looked at him.

"We have light-weight sling nets, for transferring equipment across mountainous ground. They're very strong. You can swing a mortar across a ravine that way."

"How'd you get it spread, though?"

Coggin had turned back to the window. "That street's pretty narrow," he said, "just wide enough to allow single-lane traffic. Narrow sidewalk each side. Say, eleven or twelve metres. I've got a net fifteen metres square on my truck, over at the Mission. The stays will take the weight of a mortar, like I said. We'd use the same method we do for bridging any gap in the ground. Project light-weight lines across, attached to the stays. Then draw the stays over and the net follows. Secure at four points, both sides of the road, and bob's yer uncle."

"I still want to know, how'd you get the ropes over?"

"Bolter Device," said Coggin. "It's something we adapted from a gun the Post Office uses, getting wires across freeways. Thing like an old-style cross-bow."

"A gun?"

"Sort of."

"Yeah, an' while you're firing your guns, matey, that nut will be on the way down, take my word."

"Noise isn't a problem. You can't risk noise in snowy mountains, because of the risk of avalanche. The Bolter doesn't make any more noise than a bow and arrow."

"Sounds bloody loony."

"I'd need a couple of your chaps to help. I've got five men at the Mission. We'd want at least three of us on each side."

"S'pose we could fix summink."

Mr Smail intervened for the first time. "Wouldn't you need clearance from your superiors, to use Army equipment for a civilian purpose?"

"We could get clearance."

The first fireman was staring down at the ten-storey drop. "You'd have to be sure, boy. I seen one of 'em jump once. Jewish guy, jumped off the Harbour Bridge, missed the water and hit the groyne. Split right up the middle like a paper bag. I don't want to see another like it."

"There are risks," agreed Coggin. "The police, or whoever's in charge, must decide whether to take them. Maybe they can figure a way to keep the girl's attention off us while we sling the net. The street level lights could be blacked out, and everything else below her level. Then she wouldn't even see the ropes. My boys are used to working quietly and quickly. The net's camouflaged, nothing shiny on it. Look, I don't say the idea's perfect, but what else have we got?"

Smail nodded. "I agree. I think every suggestion, however wild, must be considered. I think we should talk to Captain Finlander at once. If you'll come with me, Sergeant, I'll take you up to him."

Coggin hung back a moment, peering across the roadway to the roof of the warehouse. There was a lot he hadn't mentioned to the others; for example, that if the wind got up, or it started to snow, it might not be so simple to land the stay ropes on target. Also, in a wind, a spread net could buck like a bronco. And finally, a novice dropping into that net might well bounce or roll clean over the edge.

It would be a dangerous operation, but not as dangerous as falling ten floors to a macadam street.

Coggin set off in the wake of Mr Smail.

31

DOWN AT GROUND-LEVEL, the siege by pressmen had begun. Journalists from the city's three main newspapers were already through the police cordon, and gathered outside the main doors of Kuper's. They were giving the policeman on duty a hard time.

"Where's Finlander? When do we get a break? You know what's happened, don't you, that first story's been land-lined and it's going to hit nine o'clock television all over the country? Haven't you identified the girl yet?"

"The Captain will be down to talk to you soon."

"And the girl's identity?"

"I wouldn't know."

"I spoke to a woman back there." One of the pressmen, a bug-eyed youngster with jaws like a conger-eel, pointed at the corner of the Lane. "She told me the girl's bag bust wide open when it hit the sidewalk and there was a cheque book inside. She saw it. So the girl's name is known, right?"

"Perhaps. I wouldn't know."

The constable had run a practised eye over his tormentors. They were small-fry, but from the corner of his eye he could see the Television van edging up to the roadblock. The TV boys were something else again. The constable sighed.

He would have been even more unhappy if he had known that at that moment a woman was speaking to Phil Hackett of Cross-Country Television. Her voice was muffled. Phil decided she was disguising it.

"Do you pay," she said, "for news stories?"

Hackett flicked a switch on his intercom with one hand. He said, "There's a regulation fee for anyone who supplies us with information that provides us with material that appears on screen. Whether we pay or not is within the discretion of a senior member of staff, who doesn't happen to be me. I make no promises. What's the story?"

There was no reply. The woman appeared to be considering her options. The door to Hackett's office opened and a secretary put her head round it. Hackett flicked his right hand, signalling "Get this call on the other telephone." The secretary vanished.

"That girl on Kuper's balcony," said the voice. "I know who she is. Would you pay for that?"

"As I said, I don't decide."

Another pause. Hackett said, "If you know the woman's identity, I expect the police also know. They'll release the name in due course, so your offer has a limited life. If you want to press it, I'll have this call switched to the man who can tell you what it's worth."

"What would I get?"

"Thirty, I'd say."

"Thirty! Is that all?"

"It was enough for Jesus Christ, lady."

Hackett waited. He heard the click as the connection was broken. He sighed, replaced his receiver. The secretary came back into the room. She was a pleasant young woman, new to the job, and her face was pink with indignation.

"Do they often do that?"

"They do, love." Hackett was already reaching for the house phone. "It's our job to play along with them."

"You didn't."

"Which explains why I'll never be a Director of the Corporation. Hullo, Lew? Where's the van?"

"Stuck at the end of Manning Lane," said a petulant voice. "No traffic allowed through. Zubrowski and Liner have walked up to Kuper's and a cop says there'll be a press release soon."

"What about the warehouses?"

"James says no go. They tried to get through, across the railway lines, but the fuzz stopped them. Who is this bird, do you know? They're moving mountains for her."

"Well, she could be one of the beautiful people. I've just had an anonymous call, offering the name. Caller cried off, but left me with the feeling I should have tried harder. Can you get a message over to the boys, telling them that? Aren't there any other buildings they could work from, further up the street?"

"Nothing high enough. The Old Man knows someone who owns property on the corner, but he's out of town. It would be a bad angle, anyway, and we'd have to use telescopic."

"Well, keep trying."

"Sure."

Hackett changed over to the external 'phone. The young secretary was still staring at him.

"You mean they'd take pictures as she fell?"

"All the way down."

"It's horrible."

"Go away, girl. Go and type something."

As she quit the office, Hackett crouched over his desk. "Kuper's Stores? Phil Hackett, Cross-Country Television. I want to speak to Captain Finlander, please. I have a message for him, could be important. No, I must speak to him myself. Okay, I'll wait. As long as it takes. Thanks."

He glanced at his watch. It was still fourteen minutes till the nine o'clock news. He settled back to wait.

32

COGGIN AND FINLANDER were in an office on the eleventh floor. Finlander said, "What's the answer?"

"C.O. says he wants to get a ruling. That means Top Brass. Must be worried about something."

"Because she's a Rannault?"

"Well, he clammed up as soon as I said the name, and said he'd call me back in a quarter of an hour."

"That's quick. Means the name has a lot of pull."

"Seems like it."

The two men stared at each other appraisingly. Both had been in service long enough to know that for certain people, in certain circumstances, red tape could be cut or tied very fast indeed. Finlander said, "What's he like, your C.O.?"

"Okay. He'll fix it if he can, but he won't run the Corps into anything it can't handle."

Finlander thought that over. He decided it was going to be one of those cases when a wise policeman spoke when he was spoken to. He was not sure whether the good fairy had handed out wisdom at his cradle. Sometimes he thought what he would like to do was kick authority in the arse.

He smiled at Coggin. "Meantime, there's a Bank Manager I have to talk to. I'll be downstairs. If your call comes through, will you let me know at once?"

"Right."

Finlander went off to join Dr Lucas and Mr Flory.

33

"SHE DIDN'T RECOGNISE me." Sidney Flory, Manager of the Western and Central Bank, City Main Branch, stepped back from the balcony door with a shocked look. Behind him a voice was raised in violent abuse, shrill and hysterical. Flory shook his head, "It's incredible. I saw her only this afternoon. I've known her since she was ... why is she using that language?"

"She's sick," said Finlander, and took the manager's arm, leading him away, round the gallery and to the far side where a thin dark man leaned his elbows on the rail. Flory, recognising him, said in surprise, "Hullo, Lucas. I didn't expect to see you. My God, this is awful. Poor Ella...."

"She is Ella Rannault?"

"Of course, yes. Only this afternoon, I spoke to her." Flory caught himself on the brink of unprofessional disclosure, but Lucas prompted him.

"Tell us, Sid. It's special circumstances. Anything you can tell us may help. We know already that she drew two thousand in cash and blew the lot in a couple of hours. For an artist, I'd think that represents a pretty disturbed state of mind. It's not the highest-paid profession."

"That's no problem with Ella."

"Is her standing so high?"

"I don't know what she earns. The point is, she's a millionairess in her own right." Flory ran a hand over his hair, eyebrows flickering in indecision. "What do you want to know?"

"Anything that might tell us why she's out there," said Lucas. "We have to get near to her somehow, and quickly. She's half frozen, already. She threatened to jump when it snowed, and the storm's moving in quickly. We haven't much time."

"Yes, I see. Well. I advised her not to cash so much

money, simply because ... well ... I feel some concern for her. She has no one close to her, since her mother died. It was from her mother that she inherited, you know."

"And her father?" Finlander broke his silence. "Is he the shipping chap?"

"No, that's another branch. Ella's father is a cousin of the Coasters branch. He is interested mainly in property."

"Where does he live?"

"God knows. He travels a good deal. He could be anywhere in the world."

"What's his full name?"

"Emil Hector Rannault."

"You know him personally?"

"I knew him a long time ago. He married a local girl who was a friend of my family. Pamela Sichelle. He started with a great deal of money and multiplied it, like all his clan. They moved to the coast. There was just this one daughter. When she came back here, as an adult, she looked me up and asked me to take care of her business interests. Naturally I consented. Apart from business considerations, I felt deeply sorry for her."

"Why?" said Lucas, and Flory gave him an uneasy look.

"Emil Rannault," he said, answering at a tangent, "was a pig of a man. He was a great churchgoer, you know, sidesman, big donations to charity, but he gave his wife and child hell. Pamela was a pretty little thing without much character and Emil bullied her witless. She killed herself in the end, cut her wrists in the bath, and the child came in and found her. The child was very ill as a result. She reacted against her father, literally with violence, went for him with a knife. I'm glad to say the authorities took her out of his custody and placed her in the care of relations."

"Has she a history of mental illness?" said Lucas. "If so, I'd like to talk to someone who's treated her case."

"I can't answer that. I just know that after her mother's death she had some sort of nervous collapse. She also inherited a million in stocks and shares. She's a very ...

lonely sort of person. My wife and I have tried to include her in our circle, but she seldom responds to invitations. You can't get close to her. She has her own world, one feels. She lives her life elsewhere. I can't explain."

"You have," said Lucas.

"Because her mother committed suicide, it doesn't follow that she will, does it?"

"No. But the mother may have handed down a poor genetic heritage. The shock of her mother's death may still be expressing itself all these years later. There's a certain element of revenge present in all suicide bids, you understand? Plus self-hatred, despair, what laymen call a death-wish."

"At least," said Finlander, "we can try and get hold of her father."

"He won't help," said Flory.

Lucas nodded. "That's probably true, but we must try, useless as it probably is. From what I've heard the girl say, my guess is that she's been involved in an unhappy love affair. These people cannot make a success of human relationships, they live in a perpetual state of rejection and failure. They are continually let down by the people they hope love them. This girl's mother committed suicide. Ella will have understood that as yet another rejection, as in a sense it was. Her mother didn't care for the child enough to go on living, she killed herself and left Ella to fend for herself. Now, if there's been another let-down, by some man or woman close to her, the shock may have been great enough to pitch Ella into her second schizophrenic crisis."

Finlander was looking at his watch. "Eight-fifty-three," he said. "I have to give a Press release about nine-fifteen. I shall tell them the girl's name. If we don't get hold of her father before then, he'll very likely learn about all this from radio or TV broadcasts."

The three men started to walk back to the stairway. The Captain said, "I've a soldier, on the eleventh floor, who thinks he can sling a net across the road. He's waiting for clearance from his superiors, to use Army equipment. If he gets it, and the Press hears about it, they're going to bay like St Bernards."

"Do you think he will get it?" Flory's anxious eyes turned to the balcony door.

"Might. The Army will know that if their boy tries his act, and it doesn't come off, they'll carry the can. I can't help feeling they'll duck."

"I wish I knew her boy friend's name," said Lucas. "His full name, I mean. He's probably the only one who can save her."

As he said this, they were passing Marion Dykes. The words did nothing to ease the misery of her mind.

34

LOCKVAL HAD BEEN talking for three hours.

He had stopped thinking in any deliberate way. It seemed to him that his mind and nerves were tied to the girl's, as if they were Siamese twins. Certainly his understanding of her did not come from anything she said, because her words grew more and more incoherent as time went on. Sometimes she moaned and sometimes she shouted, leaning towards him with furious lips and blazing eyes, her hands clenched round the iron railings as if she would tear them from their stanchions.

But in this crazy tirade, he caught threads of sense; phrases that she seemed to drop by mistake, almost as if someone else spoke them when she wasn't on guard. Twice she spoke of Davey, mutterings under her breath that he should come, he was late, soon it would be too late. Once she sighed and said quietly, "I'm sorry about Paul. He'll be angry." Another time, she laughed, and when Lockval asked her why, she leered at him like an old whore and said, "Ask my father, he'll tell you." It gave Lockval an eerie feeling, the way she looked then.

Her voice was weaker than it had been. It rose and fell with the gusts of wind that blew from the north-east. As the storm moved closer, her fur coat billowed and swelled about her, her hair tossed round her face, and she raged on the narrow ledge like a demon.

Still, whenever she drew breath, whenever she was at rest for a moment, he talked to her. His even tones ran on quietly, always with an inflection of interest, of concern. His hands and face were purple with cold, and he longed to stand up and ease his limbs, but he knew that any movement could break the light link of understanding between them. Behind him, in the shadows at the back of the balcony, Milner waited, passing information to Lockval, watching the girl, ready to jump if she did; but he might have been worlds away.

"Where did you leave the note?" said Lockval to the girl, and as before she ignored the question. He tilted back his head, as if considering. "In the bathroom? That's a good place to leave a note, I'd say. On the mantelpiece, is another. In the bedroom, pinned to the pillow."

The girl was staring at him. He saw the white strained shape of her face, the half-frozen muscles pulling the cheeks and mouth out of control. She said, "I didn't look in the bathroom. I didn't look."

The intensity of her words was different from her earlier hysteria. It was as if she was defending herself against a crucial attack, repeating something she had said a thousand times.

"Why not?" said Lockval. "It's a good place to find a note."

She shook her head and her hands began to beat the rail. "No, no, no!"

"Why not?"

She bent forward and her gaze slid past him and then back with a sly and secretive air. She spoke in a whisper. "They told me I mustn't go there. But it was too late, you know. I'd already looked. She was inside, and the bath was all full of blood."

35

As Finlander entered the office, Coggin was just answering the ring of the telephone. His face screwed up in silent surprise as he listened. Then he said, "Certainly, sir," and held out the receiver to Finlander.

"Mr Van Leenveldt," he said in a dry voice, "Deputy-Secretary for Defence."

Finlander took over, and for the next few minutes listened to a voice like a rotary saw. The Ministry, having learned of the predicament of Ella Rannault, not to say Kuper's Stores, was, according to Van Leenveldt, "under severe pressure from certain quarters" to prevent publicity being given to the problem. The Press and Television must be removed from the vicinity of Manning Lane, if that were possible, and...

"It is not possible," interrupted Finlander. He was hanging on to the receiver with white knuckles, and his eyes had become diamonds of pure fury. The 'phone quacked at him and he spoke into it with acid clarity.

"It is not possible, Mr Van Leenveldt, to get rid of the Press and TV boys. Unless, of course, you want to make them sure this is a really big story they must cover at all costs? Is that your wish, sir?"

Quack, quack!

"Then perhaps you'll tell me who's trying to force a black-out, and why?"

Quack! quacketty quack!

"If I'm not kept informed, then I cannot carry out my duties. If I can't carry out my duties, the girl will jump."

Silence for a moment. Then, "This girl is probably a mental case, an hysteric. She is probably seeking publicity, and if she gets it, it may actually increase the likelihood of her ... umh ... jumping."

"The psychiatrist here," said Finlander, "believes the only way to save her is to pull in the people close to her. The only way to do that is to release her name."

"You can't do that."

"If I don't, they'll get it just the same. Someone in the crowd or elsewhere has already telephoned Cross-Country Television, offering to sell the information."

"What?" More lip-sucking. "That is very disturbing news. I think I must tell you, Captain, that this girl is not a nobody. Her father is on the P.M.'s Economic Advisory Committee, and Chairman of the National Productivity Campaign. Adverse publicity would be most unfortunate."

"I'm told," said Finlander, "that he treated the kid like dirt."

"That is mere hearsay. You will suppress such rumours with all the power at your disposal."

Finlander, who knew something of Deputies, said nothing. There were going to be other authorities with something to say about interference in police spheres. In the meantime, he wanted to know why Van Leenveldt was doing a slow boil.

The Deputy decided to come clean. "Something very disquieting has occurred," he said, "which perhaps you should know of. You have quite correctly informed your headquarters of the girl's identity, and apparently the Commanding Officer of the Fifth Mountain Corps also knows it, but I assume you have otherwise kept the covers on?"

"Correct, sir."

"The C.O., knowing the prominence of Mr Rannault's position, rang me, and I took it upon myself to ring Mr Rannault's home, which is in the capital, as you know. He was not there. I was perturbed. I know him personally, and wished to break the news about his daughter myself. I rang his office. Despite the fact that it was close to nine o'clock, the call was taken by his secretary. She informed me that she had been instructed to remain on duty, with another senior clerk, until further notice. She could not say why. She told me that just about half an hour earlier, Mr Rannault received a call from this city. He appeared to be shocked and angered by the conversation that ensued, which seemed to centre on his daughter Ella. The secretary said Mr Rannault decided to travel over here in his private jet, and left for the airport at once, taking off at about eight-fifty."

"The call didn't go from here," said Finlander. "This switchboard's monitored."

"Could some friend of Miss Rannault's have made it? Her bank manager, perhaps?"

"Perhaps. What bugs me is, why didn't her father get in touch with us here?"

"Presumably he felt that would waste time. If he left the coast at eight-fifty, he should be here very soon. I've no need to tell you, Captain Finlander, that we at the Ministry expect Mr Rannault to be received with the greatest possible..."

"Kid gloves, sir. And now, have we clearance to use the net?"

"Net? Ah, that. It sounds rather a forlorn hope. Doesn't it?"

"Sergeant Coggin is the expert. He says it's dangerous, but not as dangerous as a ten-storey fall."

"Very well. I accept that. Do what you think best, the matter is in your good hands."

"Which means," said Finlander, as he recapped the conversation for Coggin, "God help you and me if anything goes wrong. Want to chance it?"

Coggin looked at him calmly. "I've already had my men carry the stuff up from the trucks, and we've got two of them and two firemen over in the warehouse. When you're ready, we'll get cracking."

He hurried off to the ninth floor. Finlander paid a brief visit to the street. He told the pressmen assembled there that the girl on the ledge was Ella Rannault. He did not mention the long-distance call to her father, nor that Rannault was on his way to the city. But he did cross the road and tell Morrison, in the radio car, to get in touch with Police Headquarters. A police car was to meet the magnate at the airport, and bring him to Kuper's at all possible speed.

36

IT HAD GROWN quite dark in the study, except for the glow of the fire and the blue-white flicker of the television set in the corner. Deirdre rose and switched on extra lamps, but the light did not seem to bring greater clarity. Indeed it seemed to Christine, rubbing her cold hands together, that she existed outside of these everyday surroundings, that the world was going on without her while she hung in space. She said loudly, "Arnold might have woken. I should go and see." But she did not move from the window-seat, and Deirdre, having thrown a couple of logs on the fire, came back and sat down as if she had not heard.

"You don't know what it's like," said Deirdre, "until you experience it, having your whole life changed by a trivial, stupid action, something you don't even think could matter. That Christmas seemed to start so well. All the political people had cleared out for the Christmas truce. You have no idea how many of them hang around during an election, but they'd gone and we were just ourselves. We gave a New Year Party for our village friends. We decorated the barn, and that week the pond froze over, so we had skating and played silly games for the kids.

"About nine o'clock, everyone was ravenous, and I went up to the house and fetched a tray of hot pies. On the way back I met Paul and he offered to carry the tray. I could see he was very excited about something, and while I was busy piling the pies onto plates, he suddenly pulled a sheet of newspaper out of his pocket and spread it out in front of me.

"It was an advertisement placed by the Breughel Works in Germany, one of those big concerns that grew up after the war. Paul told me old man Breughel had lost his only daughter in the Dresden bombing, and wanted to set up a monument to her. 'They want the finished work, not just the design. The prize money is enough to stake me to three, maybe four years in Europe.'

"He was sure he could win, and he wasn't being immodest. The work is now in the Breughel Park in Berlin, and people from all over the world go to look at it. I was the first person to see his preliminary sketches. He showed them to me that night in the barn.

"Of course, rough drawings couldn't convey his idea fully, but I felt at once that they were important. They showed a sort of crysallis of marble, from which the figure of a young woman was about to break. In places, you could see, the rock would be as thin as silk, with the living flesh pulsing under it. From every angle, you got the impression of power and triumph, of life breaking free from ... from the immobility of death.

"Perhaps it wasn't from the drawings that I sensed this intense emotion. Perhaps it came straight from Paul's mind to mine. I believe that in the mind of a genius, the work exists as a whole, from the beginning, like a foetus. The developments that come later don't alter that elemental completeness.

"I gave the sketches back to Paul and said, 'When are you going to start?' And he said, 'As soon as you agree to model for me.'

" 'Me? You're crazy. You want a young girl.'

" 'I want the quality of vibrant life. You have it.' It was the nicest compliment that was ever paid me.

"Soon after New Year, Arnold began his election campaign. When I wasn't helping him, I'd sit for Paul. He made a clay model first. I was disappointed when I saw it, but he laughed at me. 'Clay is nothing,' he said, 'unless it's fired. In a week or two I'll destroy this. I'm just thinking aloud.'

"That was a strange few months. I lived in two worlds. I spent long stretches working with Arnold, tramping the countryside in his preliminary canvass for votes. I wrote endless envelopes, rustled up helpers, wrote manifestoes.

I believed in what Arnold was doing, I believed in political reform, and yet, all that was suddenly unimportant in comparison with the block of marble in Paul's barn. I couldn't wait to get back there, even though posing was the most exhausting thing I'd ever done. I used to sit naked and blue with cold, in spite of a ring of oil stoves all round me. Often Paul kept me sitting far too long, and Mrs November would come in and tell him to break, and give me hot drinks to get my circulation going again. She was as committed to the work as he was, and she pinned all her hopes on his winning the competition; but I was also important to the election, as the candidate's wife, and she wasn't going to spoil Arnold's chances in any way.

"By the end of May, the sittings came to an end. Paul was busy with the final polishing, and Arnold's campaign left me no time to visit the Novembers. Our house was now election headquarters. There were extra 'phones, people underfoot all day and half the night. As nomination day approached, we all ate, walked and slept politics. Arnold took leave from the city. He had the support of some big Party guns, who shared public meetings with him, and usually stayed overnight at the farm. A lot of money had been pumped into his constituency. Nobody doubted he'd win. He was terribly tired, but pleased with the way things were going, and pleased with the new vision he'd found of himself.

"'It's the most worthwhile thing I ever undertook,' he said to me one night. 'I feel close to people. I feel reborn. I'll never grudge a second of the time spent on it.'

"A couple of nights later, while Arnold was eating a late supper, a note arrived from Paul. 'It's ready. Come and see.'

"I couldn't even wait for Arnold to finish his meal, I dragged him out and made him walk across the two fields to the November's barn. There was still a hard frost, and it was like moving in a crystal ball, the smallest sound rang on the air.

"Paul was waiting in the yard, and Mr and Mrs November were there too, looking as pleased as kids. Paul said, 'It's good, Dee. It's really good. The first time I've been able to say that about anything I've done.'

"We went in. The sculpture was standing in the centre of the floor, right under the light. I went over to it and stood looking at it for a long time. It was complete, as I'd felt it in Paul's mind that first night. It was strong, simple, and very beautiful. I remembered thinking, if my child died, and I needed to believe in immortality, then this would give me what I needed.

"I turned to speak to Arnold. He was standing beside me, staring at the floor. I touched his hand and he raised his head. There was an expression of shock, fury and disgust on his face. He glared at me for a moment and then thrust me aside and rushed out of the barn. I ran after him, but he wouldn't wait. He went plunging across the fields, and I had to scramble after him as best I could. Only when we reached our own home did he speak to me.

" 'You posed for that muck, didn't you?'

"I felt dazed. I started to say something, I think I began to laugh out of sheer confusion. Arnold caught hold of my shoulders and shook me. 'You posed naked for that buck nigger to look at!'

"When he'd said that, he stopped. We stood in our hallway, and neither of us seemed able to break the silence. After what seemed a century, someone's voice sounded in the election office. It was Arnold's. They were running the tape of his last meeting. That broke the spell.

"He said, 'I'll never forgive you. You've destroyed everything for me.' He turned and walked out of the house, and he didn't come back that night or the whole of the next day.

"I nearly went crazy. We searched for him. The Party workers took over my house. There were 'phone calls, telegrams, a confidential approach to the police. And then, about eleven at night, Arnold walked in. He arrived as if nothing unusual had happened. He was calm and neat and affable. He greeted me courteously and apologised for causing me alarm. He apologised to his workers. He looked twenty years older, and his eyes were sick, but he was in complete control of himself.

"He told us that he had gone up to the city that morning, and while on his way to an interview, had suffered an attack. He implied it was a sort of black-out. He had gone straight to his doctor, who had made tests, and diagnosed 'trouble in the heart and lungs'. He had then visited Party headquarters, and held long talks with the hierarchy. It had been decided that he must withdraw from the candidacy.

"Well, there was plenty of protest and argument. The local workers thought at first they might reverse the decision, but after a while they saw it wasn't the Party bosses who were responsible. Arnold had decided to pull out and nothing was going to change his mind. There was still just time to find a substitute, and they did.

"During the next few days and weeks, I tried to reach some rational understanding, of Arnold and of myself. At last I had to accept the simple truth. Arnold recognised me as the model for Paul's work. He realised that I'd posed in the nude for a black man, and it disgusted him. It also totally destroyed his own image of himself. His liberalism was a fake. That being so, how could he pose as the champion of the black man? He was a phoney politician, and a phoney friend. If he could fail Paul in such a petty way, he'd fail others. So he did the only thing possible, he withdrew from the candidacy and got out of politics. But he never forgave me. I took too much from him.

"Paul left the village the day after he showed us the sculpture. He didn't come back until after we'd sold Crossthwaite, because of course we had to move. Arnold couldn't face the people after we let them down so badly.

"I never managed to trace Paul. Mrs November wouldn't give me his new address. She made it clear it would be best if Arnold and I kept out of her way. She and her husband understood perfectly well what had been in Arnold's mind that night. Maybe they forgave him. But it didn't leave any further basis for friendship.

"In three months, we'd found a buyer for the farm and moved back to the city. Davey suffered most. He'd loved Paul and depended on him, and Paul had gone away without even saying goodbye. He'd lost the farm. He was distraught, he wouldn't eat and he pestered us for explanations which we couldn't give. He was a child, but children are acute about people they love, and I think he knew that Paul had gone away because of a rift between Arnold and me. He blamed Arnold. He hated him. Arnold tried very hard to make it up, but of course one can't; not on any false level."

Deirdre stopped. A humming sound filled the room, the sound of the lift coming down from the upper floor. The two women rose and hurried out to the hall. Arnold Kuper was just stepping out of the lift. His face was waxen. "Deirdre! Where's David? I saw the television. Some girl is at the store, talking of suicide. I must go down there."

They tried to dissuade him, but he brushed their protests aside. "Get my coat and muffler. One of you must drive me."

Christine said, "I will."

"Very well. Deirdre?"

"I think I should stay here, Arnold. Acqbal is trying to find David. He may 'phone, or Dave might."

"Quite right. You stay."

They went off to the garage. Deirdre telephoned Marion Dykes to say they were on their way.

There were long windows on each side of the front door, and through the right-hand one she could see a little slice of the garden, snow-covered and bluish-white; and then the car, with Chris at the wheel and Arnold hunched beside her. It wound carefully between the trees and turned out of the front gate.

She wondered why she had bothered to talk to Christine. Nothing had got across.

She fetched a rug from the hall cupboard, swung an armchair close to the telephone table, and settled down to wait for Acqbal's call.

37

OVER AT THE airport, on the south-west side of the city, air-traffic had almost come to a halt. The snow storm was whirling up fast and all aircraft had been diverted to grounds further south.

One of the last 'planes to set down was a twin-engined privately-owned jet from the coast. It carried only one passenger, a barrel-chested man in a long silver-grey top-coat. He hurried across the tarmac one step ahead of his pilot and entered the reception building without looking to right or left.

He was not a particularly commanding figure, yet people cleared a path for him. His pale heavy face, pouched beside mouth and jowl, his neat silvery hair and thick glasses were somehow formidable.

The police driver sent by Finlander had literally to block the way to fix his attention.

"Mr Rannault?"

The thick spectacles swung round.

"Sir, I'm instructed to meet you and conduct you to Kuper's Stores. My name is Foster."

Rannault's mouth moved in a slow chewing movement. Then he nodded, and turned to his pilot, still following a pace behind.

"I'll go in the police car. It'll be faster. You stay here."

The pilot withdrew. Rannault returned his gaze to Foster.

"Where are you parked?"

There was no conversation during the journey across the city. The driver gave his full attention to getting through the traffic. Sometimes he used the siren. It was an experience that most people would have found interesting, but Rannault showed no emotion. He sat slumped in his seat, eyes closed, and only the constant drumming of the fingers of his left hand showed that he was not asleep.

38

ON THE NINTH floor of Kuper's, in the dim cavern of the stock-room, Sergeant Coggin and three other men were setting up their bizarre rescue operation. They could not switch on the main lights, because nothing must attract the attention of the girl on the ledge. The overhang of the balcony protected them, and the rising whine of the wind covered any sound they made.

Their first task was to secure the net on their own side of the street. It was light and easy to handle, but extremely strong, with eyeholes for the stay-ropes on all four sides.

The four men worked steadily. They anchored the net round the pilasters between the four windows, paying it out slowly from the left-hand window, which was farthest from where the girl stood. Coggin, who had never in his life experienced vertigo, swung himself along the narrow ledge between the openings and passed in the requisite stay-ropes. Once these were fixed in place, the slack of the net was taken up in neat concertina folds, along the side of the building, so that in due course it could be drawn without hitch across the road.

Finally the free ends of the stay-ropes on the other side of the net were fitted into socket-grips. These sockets were attached to nylon fishing-line tough enough to land a giant tunny, the line being coiled on a king-sized reel. Coggin picked up one of the reels in his hand and showed it to the fireman, Harris, who was one of his team.

"This is part of the Bolter Device," he said. He stooped and came up with a thing like a mediaeval cross-bow, except that the frame was aluminium, with a very competent trigger arrangement.

"The reel fits so," said Coggin, locking it in place. "The

bow's not difficult to handle. You grip it like this." He stood behind the fireman, demonstrating. "Got the idea? You sight along here. Up a little; the drag will cause the rope to drop, and we have to be sure we hit the warehouse roof first time. You done Army service?"

"Yeah."

"Then the trigger's the same as on a rifle. Squeeze, don't snatch, and the lady's all yours. Right?"

"Right." The fireman sounded more confident than he felt. He stood at the window, checking the weight and sight of the mechanism. Coggin watched for a moment, and then turned to the other men.

"The warehouse," he said, "is flat, and there are those two big chimney-stacks you can see sticking up. They'll act as bollards for the stays on that side. We've got two soldiers and two firemen over there. Kaplan's in charge. The roof's a big higher than we are here, so the net's going to slope down towards us. They'll have to leave a little slackness in it, or it'll act like a trampoline. Now. It's going to take the lads on the other side two or three minutes to grab the stays, pull the net over, secure it. They'll have to move carefully or the girl will spot them Luckily the balustrade is high and solid, it'll give them cover. Still, that two or three minutes is the critical period. The police boys are going to try and hold the girl's attention long enough for us to do the job, so we'll take up stations and go when they say so.

"That wind can muck it," said one of the soldiers, and Coggin nodded.

"It won't help, but we've managed worse. Joe, it's a four metre drop from the ledge to where the net will be. She could roll off. As soon as she hits, I'm going out there to grab her. If I need help, you follow."

"Right."

Fireman Harris was leaning forward to peer from the window. "Christ," he said, and drew back, looking green. "How'll you know when to begin?"

"There's a night-guard called Bronson. Captain Finlander will send him down to tell us. We can't use walkie-talkie, she might hear."

They settled down to wait, one man at each window, like archers at the embrasures of a fortress.

39

ELAINE BONDI WAS on the eleventh floor, in an office well-removed from the central management suite used by Finlander a while earlier.

She had switched on a single desk lamp, and sat in a swivel-chair, the telephone on her lap. There was something both eager and furtive in her crouched attitude. Close to her on the floor lay a sheet of foolscap bearing a list of names and addresses, and from time to time she leaned over to study this. At the moment she was busy dialling. She did not notice the man in the corridor outside, but he observed all her actions with close interest.

"Mr Tyzack?" Elaine spun the chair a little to the right, as if that might put an extra degree of persuasion into her voice. "Elaine Bondi here. I'm speaking on behalf of Mr Booth, Mr Tyzack. We're very anxious to get hold of Mr David Kuper. He's not at his home, nor at Mr Arnold's house, and we wondered if perhaps he might have called round to see you? Well, yes, it is urgent. No, of course, if you have no knowledge ... of course. I'm sorry to have bothered you. If he does show up, would you ask him to 'phone the store at once? Extension 2071. Thank you very much, Mr Tyzack. Good-night."

As Elaine depressed the receiver, the man in the corridor stepped forward. She heard the footfall and swung round with a cry of fright. When she saw who it was, the Madonna cheeks plumped in a smile. "Oh, Mr Booth. You did give me a scare!"

"I'm sure I did, my dear." Booth held a cigar in one hand, and he raised it to his lips, watching her as he puffed smoke aside. "After all, you're taking my name in vain, aren't you? I don't remember asking you to 'phone the Board members."

The young woman flushed. "I thought it was important to find Mr Kuper."

"Very enterprising."

She stared up at him with narrowed eyes, trying to gauge the emotion behind his bland gaze. "I think David should be here. He's the owner's son after all, and if Mr Arnold is too ill to come himself..."

Booth laid the cigar in an ashtray on the desk, and slowly dusted his palms together. "Elaine, my child, it would be better if you were frank with me."

"I am, Mr Booth. I'm trying to help."

"I'm sure you are, but whom? There have been some very strange events here today. I must tell you that I instructed the man on the switchboard to keep an ear on outgoing as well as incoming calls. He tells me that a short while ago, someone 'phoned Cross-Country Television and offered to sell them the name of that girl on the balcony. The voice was disguised, as if the person spoke through a handkerchief. The extension line used was this one."

"What a dreadful thing! It must have been only a little while before I got here. I saw the light was on, and when I found this line was connected, I used it myself. Why would anyone want to do such a mean thing?"

"Money," said Booth. "But I guess in this case the rewards of treachery seemed too slight. A pity you didn't arrive up here a little sooner. Now we shall never know who made the call, hmh?" He smiled. "As to David, it's no good chasing him. I've already 'phoned every member of the Board. Tried his Clubs, his favourite dives, one or two of his ... ah ... lesser-known cronies. He's nowhere to be found. Odd, I admit. But why don't we just assume that he does not wish to be found? Why don't we just wait and see what happens?"

Elaine continued to study him. She had the look of a cornered cat that wonders whether to claw or run. "He'll have some explaining to do, if it turns out he knew that girl."

"Knew? Why the past tense? She's still alive."

"She'll jump," said Elaine coolly.

"You're a bloody cold fish, aren't you?"

"I face facts. Sooner or later she'll kill herself. That's what she believes herself, so one day it will happen."

"Then let us hope this is neither the hour nor the place." Booth picked up his cigar again and gently touched off the ash. "Why are you so sure David knows her?"

"She got into Soft Furnishings through the emergency door. That means she had a set of control keys. I saw them in the balcony door, before the police took them. There's a turquoise stone on the ring, like the one David Kuper has. I didn't think of it straight away, then I realised the girl must be pretty close to him to be able to steal his keys. He always carried them on him."

"And like the discreet little puss that you are, you said nothing to anyone? Well, discretion saved many a cat from the skinner."

Malice sparked in her eyes. "I have to be discreet, Mr Booth. I hear a lot of things. For instance, someone told me the other day that Sizzle wanted to amalgamate with Kuper's. This person said there were people on our Board who wouldn't resist a move like that. If Mr Arnold got to hear of it, there might be a lot of trouble, mightn't there, but I know how to hold my tongue."

She stood up, collecting her purse and the typed list. Booth watched her, chin on chest. As she walked past him, he dropped an arm round her shoulders, halting her.

"Don't think I don't appreciate you, my dear. I merely warn you against penny-snatching. The sale of information is seldom lucrative ... or safe."

He turned her round and began to stroll with her towards the door. "Now if you want a good investment, tell Sam to buy a thousand of the new Pradura issues tomorrow. They'll open at 250 and double quite quickly.

"Really? Thanks for the tip, Mr Booth. We'll do as you say."

In all matters concerning profit and loss, Elaine Bondi and Deryk Booth shared a perfect understanding.

40

MARION DYKES REPLACED the receiver and said, "Thank God for that." As Barry Teale looked at her enquiringly, she said, "Arnold Kuper is coming in. His daughter-in-law Christine will bring him."

She sank into a chair near the counter. "I shouldn't be glad, really. He isn't well enough to be subjected to strain like this, but if he wants to come ... he loves the store, it's been his life's work ... if something dreadful happens ... then I'd rather he was here."

Teale studied her quietly for a moment, and then said, "By something dreadful, you mean something other than the girl's suicide?"

She met his eyes. "That must sound very strange to you. It is strange, that anything should seem more important than death; but I'm being honest. There are people and subjects that matter more to me than the girl does."

"What are you afraid of?"

"I don't know." She wrapped her arms round herself and glanced up at the balcony. The icy air poured through the open doors. "I'm so cold."

Teale moved to the shelves beneath the counter, and lifted out a bolt of heavy tweed. He jerked several lengths of material free, and swung them round Miss Dykes' knees.

"Sit quietly for a while. You've suffered a great shock. Everyone is shocked, and cold, I should have had the sense to do something about it long ago. There's a canteen over at the Mission and I am going to ask them to send over hot food and drinks for everyone."

"You won't tell them what's happening, will you?"

"I won't. But I think, you know, Ella Rannault is public property by now. Rest a little, why don't you? I'll be back."

Miss Dykes leaned sideways against the counter, pulling a fold of tweed round her shoulders. She was thinking of the Kupers. They'd be halfway here by now. Had anyone warned them that this girl might be David's mistress? Could one suggest such a thing, unless one was sure of one's ground?

And yet ... it was no use quibbling ... everyone had known for years that David was a womaniser. There'd been gossip, but no open scandal. But then, none of his women had ever threatened to jump off a skyscraper.

It was no use panicking. One must think, and try to minimise the damage. Protect Arnold. He was strait-laced and proud, scandal would be hell for him. He'd worry so, about the effect on the store, on David.

He'd worry most of all about Christine.

Miss Dykes realised this last fact with astonishment. She considered it, sitting in her grotesque drapery of tweed, with the calmness of emotional exhaustion; Arnold loves Christine.

Tonight, at this time of crisis it was not Deirdre who was bringing him to the store, but Chris. There came to her mind, like shell-bursts in a dark sky, pictures of the Kuper family, and she thought, The truth has been under our noses, all these years, and we've ignored it because ignorance was more comfortable and more advantageous.

And if I see it now, she thought, surely Deirdre must have seen it long ago, and David too?

How they must have suffered, all of them.

"You're pale as a ghost." Teale was at her side, looking concerned. "I've ordered everything hot the canteen provides. Now I must fix it so my staff have permission to fetch it up here. At least we'll not go supperless."

He started to move away, but Marion, struck by another idea, seized his arm. "Mr Teale. One moment. You said, earlier, that you'd met Deryk Booth before. Can you remember where?"

"Yes certainly. It was at Santos and Liveridge. They look after the Mission's legal business."

"Was this recently?"

"Oh no. Some time last year, I think. I called in to discuss some Church matter and Mr Booth was there. He greeted me most affably and told me he'd been arranging a stop-order grant in favour of the Mission. It turned out to be very generous. That's why I remembered the occasion."

"I see. Thank you." Miss Dykes rose. "I must go and tidy. Arnold Kuper will be here shortly. I hope, if you've a moment, you'll allow me to introduce him to you?"

"It will be a pleasure. We've been neighbours, in a manner of speaking, for years."

She gave a funny little ducking bow which Teale recognised as dismissal. Strange woman. She had for a short time needed help, and now she did not. Probably she was already ashamed of her passing weakness; for that's how she would view confession.

She was already stumping off towards the foyer. Teale bent and retrieved the tangled lengths of tweed, and, first smoothing them on the counter, returned them neatly to the bolt.

41

ABOUT TEN MINUTES after Arnold and Christine Kuper had left the house, Deirdre heard a car turn through the gates at the foot of the park. Through the window, she watched a station-wagon spurting up the driveway, its headlights glinting on points of ice. She opened the front door and stood shivering at the top of the steps.

The wagon swung round the turning-circle and stopped. The driver hurried towards her.

"Deirdre, I'm sorry. I didn't have time to warn you..."

"It's all right. Acqbal 'phoned me. Come in."

As he approached, she peered at him closely. The half-light from the doorway gave his face the exaggerations of a tribal mask, beaked nose and slanted, cavernous eyes. She turned without a word and led him into the house.

"Go over to the fire," she said as they entered the drawing-room. "I'll mix you a drink. What would you like?"

"Brandy, please."

He sat close to the hearth, his big hands held out to the flames, and she saw the ridged callouses along the edge of his palms, the mark of his trade. She carried a glass over to him and he looked up and smiled as he took it. Only then did she realise that there had been no formal greeting between them. Across a gap of twenty years, he had needed no bridge of conventional speech. He had changed very little in that time. His presence still dominated the space around him. His big frame in its black overalls seemed vibrant against the flat dimensions and careful colours of this room. He must by now be used to attention and fame. He had all the power of wealth and of recognised genius. Yet his voice was gentle and diffident.

"I've been wondering all day," he said, "whether to come and talk to you. This didn't seem the time to stand on ceremony, so when Acky called..."

"I'm glad you're here."

"You're alone?"

"Yes. Christine ... that's David's wife ... and Arnold have gone down to the store."

"And David?"

"No one knows." She sat down on the opposite side of the hearth. "He didn't sleep at home last night. He hasn't been home today, or to the office."

"I know." The black man looked at her carefully. "This girl. Ella Rannault. She's kind of a friend of his."

"You don't have to be tactful with me, Paul. You mean she's his mistress?"

"Yes. He was with her last night."

"I see. Well, if it's a question of an affair, even a divorce, that's something one can face, surely? Why must David hide away like this?"

"It's more than an affair, Dee."

She looked puzzled. "Love, then?"

"There's no love as you know it."

"I don't understand. I'm ... I'm rather muddled tonight, you'll just have to explain everything to me as if I was a half-wit."

He leaned forward, elbows on knees, and spread his hands in a groping gesture. "I blame myself for David's trouble," he said. "I don't think he knows anything about love and that's maybe because I let him down. You know ... after I left Crossthwaite that time ... he wrote to me? He gave the letter to my mother and she sent it on. Did he tell you that?"

"No."

"Figures, I suppose. Anyway, after a time I wrote back giving my new address. Every now and again he'd send a letter, the stuff kids write. He hated that school you chose for him, in town."

'He'd have been unhappy anywhere."

"Maybe, but some places could have taught him to come to terms with himself. Anyway, after I won the Breughel Prize, I went to Europe. He still wrote. Sometimes he'd send me some of his drawings. Tell me things that bothered him in his painting, or at school. He never mentioned home. I was sorry. I'd have liked to have news of you. I've read all your books." He lifted his head and gave his slow smile. "Thought one day you'd put me in one, make me famous; but you never did."

"I never needed to exorcise you."

"Is that the way it works? In that case, I'm glad. Well. After a while David's letters stopped coming. I decided it was best to leave it so. I thought he'd heal quicker if I wasn't in his mind. When I came back from Italy ... that was four years ago ... I looked him up. He was in business, seemed happy enough, but not particularly keen to renew acquaintances."

"I expect he was jealous of you. He tried to make a living as a painter, you see, but the critics panned him. That's when he decided to go into Kuper's."

"Then he was a fool."

"It's easy for you to say. You're successful."

"Now, yes. It took time. But Deirdre, you know that's not the point. The only person an artist has to be good enough for is himself. The opinion of a critic isn't worth a damn. It can't add anything and it can't take anything away. This scale of success and failure we judge by ... it's a murderous thing. It's what's put Ella Rannault on that ledge tonight, and David God knows where. I've been going crazy this afternoon, looking for him."

Deirdre straightened up with a look of sharp challenge. "What do you mean, this afternoon? That girl only got out on the balcony at 6.20."

"I know." Paul's gaze shifted to his hands. "It's pretty complicated. I'll tell it from the beginning. I've known Ella several years. A doctor I know came to me, soon after I got back, and said would I give a couple of talks at the mental hospital over at Lafitte. Perhaps give a few lessons in how to model clay. He said it was occupational therapy for depressed patients. Ella was one of those. She was in the hospital as a voluntary case, and she was already close to being discharged.

"I used to meet her in the workrooms up there. I knew straight away she was a trained artist. The doctor showed me some things she'd painted while she was sick. Queer, disjointed things, but she knew how to use paint, and as she responded to treatment, the pictures began to pull together, too. We'd talk about her work, and mine. I got to know her quite well. You can't say we were friends. Ella doesn't have friends, she doesn't know how. There's a wide moat round her, but she likes to talk across it sometimes.

"She has never mentioned her family to me, although the doc said her father is alive. She lives in a house on Whytewych Dock, nobody else in it except an old woman called Mrs Samuels who caretakes, cleans the place and looks after it if Ella is away.

"She doesn't have to work for a living. Her father is a multi-millionaire, and she inherited over a million of her own, from her mother. Yet each Christmas, when Kuper's takes on temporary commercial artists, Ella goes along and signs on. At first she liked the company. Now I know she doesn't even notice company. There's only one person in the store, perhaps the world, she gives a hoot for, and that's David.

"Deirdre, you know how a grown man or woman can have a sort of love affair in their mind? Love someone they've never spoken to, never met? They can create a whole secret life for themselves, know what I mean? Ella was like that. She loved David. I believe if she'd never met him, but just gone on loving him in her fantasy world, then she'd have been safe; but she did meet him, and it was my fault.

"When she was discharged from hospital, I began selling her the idea she must plan her own show of work. She'd done some fine landscapes, and a couple of good abstracts. I told her to keep building up a collection. It took her two years, and in August last, I helped her to fix her exhibition at Yerbin Acqbal's gallery.

"It was advertised, and we got a paragraph in the paper, announcing the opening. A couple of nights before, David rang me and said he'd been sent a ticket. He'd seen something of Ella's and liked it. He'd be there.

"He came to the opening, and of course we talked. He liked the collection, bought one picture, and asked to meet Ella. I looked around for her but couldn't see her. The place was full of people squawking and guzzling cheese and wine, but Ella had vanished. Acky, when I managed to get hold of him, said she'd felt sick and left. It was no surprise. She'd get these moods and just walk out.

"I went back and told David. He said, 'Well, if she's gone home, let's go there.'

"'She's sick,' I said. 'She won't want visitors.'

"'Probably she was just fed up with this mob.'

"I argued with him, but he was absolutely determined to meet Ella, and as he was a potential client, I didn't want to brush him off too hard. So eventually the two of us went down to Whytewych. When we got there, David talked Mrs Samuels into letting us into the house, and he talked me into going up with him to knock on Ella's door. I suppose by that time I was just taking the line of least resistance.

"Ella answered the tenth knock. She came and opened the door and stood there staring at David as if she'd seen a ghost, and then she turned to me and said, 'You shouldn't have brought him, Paul.' Looking at her, I realised she was scared. She thought David in the flesh was going to destroy the dream she'd built. David took no notice of the way she behaved. He kept telling her how terrific her collection was, and in the end Ella just sort of shrugged and asked us in.

"That was a pretty awful evening. We sat in the living-room and drank vodka and coffee. David talked, I tried to, Ella hardly uttered a word. She was like a twelve-year-old kid, in an agony of embarrassment, she stared past us as if we weren't there and yet you could tell she was so much aware of David it was torturing her.

"When we left, David walked with me down to the Dock, where we'd left our cars. He said Ella 'fascinated' him. She was 'unusually talented, mixed-up of course, but intelligent and also beautiful'. I'd heard enough of the gossip to know that Dave wasn't exactly settled in his marriage and liked picking up girls. I told him straight out not to try any games with Ella. I said she'd had a lousy childhood, that since then she'd been in and out of mental homes, and although she was okay at the moment, she was about as tough as a piece of rice-paper.

"He said I mustn't worry. He knew all about Emil Rannault, and what a bastard he was. He said it would be a pleasure to give Ella a start, buy some of her pictures and see that other well-heeled citizens did the same.

"Nothing I said put him off. His mind was set on getting to know Ella. Next day, he sent her flowers. Lily of the valley in a white tub. Next time I called to see her, he was there, looking as if he'd been her childhood companion. So it began. Dave must have known quite early that Ella was living a dream about him. He didn't try to straighten her out. In fact, he encouraged her in every way he could. He seemed to be as deep in love as she was. That September, I had to go away to Paris. When I came back, they were sleeping together. Ella was twenty-seven years old, but I'm sure she'd never had a man before. She was entirely vulnerable. It was no good talking to her, so I talked to Dave again.

"I used some hard words. I told him if he cheated Ella, she might well end her days in an asylum. He told me to mind my own business. She'd never had any happiness, and he was giving her happiness, and she was free, white, and twenty-one and could look after herself.

"The thing that scared me was that I agreed with him. I've told you Ella is unbalanced, but you must understand that she is also extremely clever, in some ways. She has her father's shrewdness about practical things, money in particular. When David talked about his career, about Kuper's, she was right on his ground. She made it her concern to learn all she could about his work, and the set-up at the store. She knew Arnold Kuper was ill, and she told me calmly once that David wanted to take over from his father, but some of the Board members were blocking him because he was too young.

"She was interested in anything connected with David. She used to talk to me, and ask me about his childhood. She made me describe his family, his wife, the things he liked. I could see she was storing away every detail in her mind, the way women do when they're in love.

"Yet all the time she was loving him and treasuring him, she was also watching him. There was a cold part of her mind that wasn't fooled. Sometimes, when I was with them, David would talk about his plans for developing Kuper's, how he wanted to expand but the city was short of land in the central sector, and maybe he'd have to decentralise. Ella would sit watchful and silent, and I got the feeling that what she was thinking was somehow very dangerous.

"You see, the strain of the affair was already too much for her. Her health was deteriorating every day. She was as thin as a knife, nervous, burned up with restless energy. She did hardly any painting. David was restless too. I was convinced he wasn't happy with Ella. The only thing they had going for them was sex, and out of bed they were bad-tempered strangers. I didn't enjoy being with them, and the only reason I kept on going to Whytewych was because Ella insisted. In a queer sort of way I felt she wanted me as a witness. She loved David, but she didn't trust him. She was collecting stories about him because she loved him, and at the same time she was collecting facts that told against him. One part of her was getting ready for the moment when he double-crossed her, and when that happened, she'd act."

Paul November stopped talking and silence seemed to spread away from him, engulfing Deirdre, the room, the house. Deirdre found herself listening for a footfall. She shook her head wildly, as if to free herself from nightmare. "Act? For God's sake, Paul, what are you trying to say?"

"That Ella is a lonely woman, who never had an ounce of love in her life until she met Dave. That she's a very rich woman, with the sort of influence that goes with money. That if she ever got the idea Dave was trying to use her, she could turn against him and do him a serious injury."

"You mean hurt him? Kill him?"

"Oh God, no. I'm sure there's no violence in Ella. She could damage him in other ways. Like I said, she has great influence. Her father owns half this city."

Deirdre's lips moved as if she were trying to marshall her wits. At last she said, "You said Dave was trying to use her. Why did you say that?"

"It's nothing I know, only what I feel. The past few days, Ella has been very depressed. Yesterday evening I went down to Whytewych to see her, and found a change.

She was very ... uplifted and strange. As if she'd come to a decision, I reckon. When I said good-night to her, about nine o'clock, she told me she might not see me again to wish me a happy Christmas. She said, 'I'm going to have things out with Davey. If he cares for me, he'll leave his wife for me. It it's only the land he wants, then he's finished.' The way she spoke, frightened me. As I was walking down Hogg Lane, I bumped into David. I told him not to go and see Ella, because she wasn't well, but he just laughed. He said, 'I've burned my boats, Paul. I can't go home tonight, and I don't intend to sleep rough, so I'll take my chances up there.'

"This morning early I went up to Ella's again. Mrs Samuels answered the door and told me nobody was awake upstairs yet. I went down to the yacht basin and spent the morning working on my boat, but I couldn't get Ella and Dave out of my mind. I went back. This time the old lady said both of them had left the house. She's not very observant, sits over the TV all day, but she did say that Ella went out about ten, and David a couple of hours later. He rushed out of the house, she said, 'Like he was running for the last train.'

"I 'phoned Kuper's and they told me Dave hadn't appeared. I tried his home and got a daily help, who said Miss Christine was out. I couldn't leave a message with the daily. I tried other places Dave might have gone, and twice I went back to Whytewych in case Ella had turned up. The last time was late afternoon, and I made Mrs Samuels take me up to Ella's flat. The bed hadn't been made, and there was some sort of stuff on the looking-glass, as if someone had written a message and scrubbed it off, not very thoroughly.

"I waited at the flat about an hour and a half. It was dark and the storm coming up. Finally, about seven-thirty, I decided to go up town and get something to eat. I was crossing Parade Square when I saw the crowd in Porter's Way. There was a police van blocking access to Manning Lane. People in the crowd said there was someone on a ledge outside Kuper's. I went right round the store to the west end of the Lane. There was another block there, but a smaller crowd. Again I got the same story, a woman on the ledge, threatening suicide. I was sure it was Ella. I walked back to Parade Square, trying to think what to do. I knew it was no use looking for Dave, he'd gone to ground somewhere. I went into a hotel on the Square and put through a long-distance call to Ella's father. I told him about the woman on Kuper's balcony, and said I thought it might be Ella. He didn't seen surprised. Only angry. He said he'd come over to the city straight away, but would I please keep my ideas to myself."

"Do you think someone had already tipped him off?"

"No. But I think he knows something we don't."

"About Dave?"

"Maybe. Anyway, he wasn't going to discuss it with me. He hung up and I went home to my own apartment. I was having something to eat when Acky 'phoned me. He said you were anxious about Dave and wanted to get hold of me. Said you knew about Ella trying to kill herself. So I told him I'd come over and see you. That's all, I guess, Dee. I don't know how I can help you, but if you can think of a way, just say."

"Would you just stay and keep me company? I don't think I can stand waiting here alone."

"Sure." He smiled at her. "Shall I mix us a couple of drinks?"

"Good idea."

He moved to the bar-table. Her next question caught him off guard.

"Why was Ella Rannault in the nursing-home?"

"She was ill. Depressed. I think she tried to gas herself in a motor-car, but someone found her in time."

"She wasn't violent? She never tried to ... to hurt anyone?"

"Oh God, no." He hurried back to her. "No, Dee, put that idea out of your head. Ella never harmed anyone, I'm sure of it."

"But she is mad," said Deirdre. "How do you know what a mad person will do?"

42

TARBOTEN AND QUINCEY were in Ella Rannault's living-room, with old Mrs Samuels. Tarboten stood over by the window, keeping out of her line of vision, and she had forgotten about him. Quincey sat on the sofa, and the old woman sat next to him, scanning his face as he talked. Now she said, "I don' want anyone should get in trouble."

"Nobody blames you, Mrs Samuels. Just tell me quietly, do you think Miss Rannault wrote something on the mirror in there?"

"She did sometimes."

"Write messages? In soap, something like that?"

"Yes."

"For her friend to read?"

"For anyone. Me, anyone. Don' know why she must use the glass, plenty of paper she could use."

"Was the message there yesterday when you cleaned the flat?"

"No."

"So it was written last night or today?"

Thin shoulders shrugged.

"Tell me Gran, you know the name of the man who slept here last night?"

"I don' know."

"But if he was here often..."

"I mind my business." Her tone was categoric. "I went to my own room half past eight, I shut the door, what Miss Rannault does is for her and God to judge."

Memory nudged Quincey into a sudden guess. "Is it a black man? A black man who wears a track suit?"

"Nothing to do with him! He's a good man!"

"Okay. He's a good man, but is he a friend of Miss Rannault?"

She stared at him tight-lipped and he saw that there were tears in her eyes. He smiled at her.

"Gran, you can't change things. We'll find out sooner or later. Meantime, there's a girl out there close to death. Maybe she needs her friends, and maybe those friends would like to know about her trouble, so they can help?"

She shook her head at him.

"All right. Forget that one. Tell us about the man who stayed last night. You know his name?"

"It wasn't Mr November!" She pounded the sofa with a bony fist. "You make sure of that. It wasn't him."

"Is Mr November the black man?"

"He's a fine man. He was the only one who was always good to her. He'd come round here when she was in a bad way, like she was sometimes, and talk to her. He helped a lot of people. When I was sick he did all my shopping and fixed up about my pension."

"He called here this afternoon, didn't he?"

"Yes. He came here three times today, worrying about her, where was she, had she 'phoned? Early this morning, and about noon, and again this evening."

"Do you think he knew she planned to kill herself?"

Another shrug.

"But he was worried about her this morning?"

"And last night. He came round specially to see her. He was talking up there a long time. About nine o'clock he came down the stairs and she stood up on the landing. I heard him tell her, 'Talk to David, Ella. Get it out in the open, make him tell you the truth and take it on from there.' But she just laughed, the crazy way she has. He went away, and then the other one came."

"The one called David?"

"That's right. Up he went, like he owned the place. Then they were shoutin', you could hear them through the door, even. And the music too. Then I guess they went to bed. That's how they were. Cats, fightin' and sinnin' in that bed. God will judge them, I say."

"This David. You don't know his other name?"

"No."
"He stayed all night?"
"Must have, mustn't he?"
"Why?"
"Because I heard him leave this mornin'. First she went out, ten o'clock, same as always. Then about twelve, he went. Down the stairs, across the terrace, and off."
"Did he have a car?"
"Oh yes. But you can't bring a car up Hogg Lane. He always left it down by the Dock. In the garage."
"Which garage?"
"Behind Gregg's Boathouse. There's a lot of people use the sheds down there."
"Mrs Samuels, you said Miss Rannault always went out at ten o'clock. Do you know where she went?"
"Sure. She did her shopping."
"Did you see her go out yesterday?"
"Yes."
"What was she wearing?"
The old woman considered. "That pink suit with a grey line. She looked smart. I told her, 'You look smart.' "
"Did she have a shopping bag with her?"
"A basket, like always."
"Did she usually bring the marketing home?"
"Sure. Who wants to lug the potatoes round town?"
"But yesterday she didn't come back?"
"That's right."
"You weren't surprised?"
"I mind my business. I can't worry what she does. She's crazy anyhow."
There seemed to be no more the old woman could or would tell them. They let her go back to her television set. Quincey put through a call to Kuper's Stores and told Finlander that Miss Rannault had a close friend named Paul November, and another named Dave, surname unknown.
This done he looked at Tarboten. "We've overstayed our unofficial welcome, chum. We better go."

Tarboten was frowning. "She writes a suicide threat on the mirror, pinches her boyfriend's keys, and goes off to do a bit of shopping? It doesn't look right to me."

Quincey nodded. "Something else. It's his personal key-ring. Finlander told me someone at the store identified it. So it has his car-key on it, and the key to his garage and the lot. What would you do if someone pinched the key of your car?"

"'Phone for the spare to be brought to me."

"That's right. I think we should go down and take a look at that garage."

They left the house in Franz Place and walked down the hill towards the Yacht Basin.

43

"I COULD TELL them to sling the net now," said Finlander, "and take a chance she won't notice."

He stood with Lucas at the balcony doors. They stared at the girl on the ledge, wraithlike against the yellow sky, her thin hair glinting with snow-crystals.

"She's breaking up very fast," said Lucas. "I think you must take the risk."

Finlander nodded. As he turned to the stairs, Marion Dykes, who had been standing just behind him, caught at his sleeve.

"Captain. I heard what you said. I think I know a way to help."

The two men looked at her. She seemed half-crazy herself, her hands and lips trembling uncontrollably. "I should have spoken before," she said. "I should have said. ... Mrs Kuper, Mrs David Kuper will be here very soon. I think you must ask her to talk to the girl."

"Why?" Finlander's voice was sharp, and Miss Dykes blinked up at him, but she answered steadily enough.

"David Kuper knew her. I think, perhaps, they've been sleeping together."

"Why in hell didn't you tell us earlier?"

"I know. I'm sorry. I've been in turmoil. One doesn't like to suggest such a thing without proof."

Finlander turned his back on her. "Doc? What do you think? Would she talk to the wife?"

Lucas frowned. "She might. She's hardly listening to Lockval now. But some very powerful emotion might jerk her back to us. It's worth trying."

"Okay. As soon as Mrs Kuper arrives, I'll speak to her."

Miss Dykes made a small sound of distress and the men glanced at her. She said, "What if Christine doesn't know about the girl?"

"She'll know soon enough, whatever happens. I'd say she'd rather hear it from me than read it in tomorrow's papers."

Miss Dykes moved away. Down on the show-room floor Barry Teale was dispensing bowls of soup and hot dogs. Deryk Booth and Elaine Bondi were there, with Bronson and the caretaker. Marion did not join them, but walked quietly over to the elevator foyer to wait for Arnold and Christine.

44

ARNOLD KUPER WAS dragging every breath from the soles of his feet. He was grey and sweating. As he stepped from the elevator, Christine put an arm round him.

"Please let me send you home. I'll stay."

He shook his head. The pressure of his fingers told her to go forward, and she obeyed, her arm supporting his weight, her gaze hostile to the people moving towards them. Marion Dykes reached them first.

"Arnold! I must warn you..."

But she never had time to complete her sentence. Booth, Elaine Bondi, and a senior police officer approached together. Arnold extended a hand to the policeman. Christine said in a loud voice, "I am Mrs David Kuper. This is Arnold Kuper, my father-in-law. He shouldn't talk too much. He shouldn't be here."

"Now, Chris." Arnold was straightening his back, mustering a smile. Finlander smiled back.

"Sir, Mrs Kuper's right. You don't look too well. Why don't you go and sit down in the show-room for a while? I'd like a few words with Mrs Kuper, anyway."

"Say them here," said Christine. "I'm staying with Arnold."

But the other man pushed her gently from him. "Do as you're asked, Chris."

She gave him a glance bright with tears, and then swung round to face Finlander.

"All right. But hurry."

"Will you come over here, ma'am? I'd like you to meet Dr Lucas. He thinks you can help us."

"All right." She followed him unwillingly to the foot of the gallery stairs, where Lucas was waiting.

Arnold Kuper turned to Marion and took her arm. She began to lead him slowly across the show-room floor to the chairs placed ready. He stood for a moment staring intently at the open doors of the balcony, then settled back with a sigh.

"How is she?"

Booth spoke. "Still out there, but getting crazier by the minute."

"Her name is Rannault? Is that Emil Rannault's daughter?"

"That's right. You know her?"

"Not personally." Arnold laid a hand to his chest and drew a difficult breath. "Know of her. Painter, umh?"

"Yes."

"Does Rannault know?"

"Yes. He's on his way here."

"Good. Anything we can do?"

"Nothing."

Marion cut in suddenly. "Do you know where David is?"

"No. Chris told me in the car ... they quarrelled last evening. He hasn't been home since. Chris says, this girl may be his mistress. Don't worry, I understand the situation. We'll weather it."

He met Marion's eyes and read in them some urgent message. He hesitated a moment, and then said "Deryk, Elaine, would you oblige me? Deryk, if you'd go down to the door to wait for Rannault? Courtesy, uhm? And Elaine. In my desk, bottom right drawer, a hand atomiser? Help. Would you?"

The two hurried away. Arnold's tired eyes lifted again to Marion.

"Well?"

"David's missing, Arnold."

"I imagine ... he'll turn up ... when the trouble's over. As usual."

"But what if he's involved in something really wrong? Oh, not that girl, nobody worries about things like that nowadays. But something else?"

"Such as?"

"Booth." Marion came quickly to the chair next to his and sat leaning forward, her fists clenched on her knees. "Arnold, there's something going on. Deryk's up to something. He's involved David. I'm sure of it." The words tumbled out with increasing intensity. "He's disloyal to you, Arnold. He's ambitious, he's only waiting for your shoes, he'd do anything to push you aside, and he'll do the same to David, only David doesn't see it any more than you do. Booth would like to see David in the mud, that would serve his purpose, as long as it didn't brush off onto him."

Arnold's eyes had strayed from her to the gallery. He was looking up with great anxiety. "They won't let Chris go out there, will they? That woman might be dangerous."

"Listen to me." Miss Dykes beat her fists on her thighs. "You've never listened. I've warned you. Barry Teale knows Deryk, he met him at the lawyers that look after the Mission business. Deryk said he'd come there to make a grant to the Church. Why? He's never given anything to anyone unless there was something in it for himself. He's as mean as hell, you know that."

"Maybe he's trying to save his soul." When Arnold smiled, his face had great charm, but Miss Dykes was beyond being charmed.

"You fool," she said. "If they've got hold of the Mission land, then you can say goodbye to..."

"Hush," said Arnold, laying his hand on her wrist. "Rannault's arrived. We can talk later."

45

"You may feel we're asking too much of you," said Lucas.

The blonde woman did not appear to hear him. Her head was turned away. She was watching Arnold Kuper with an anxious and protective expression.

"Do we ask too much?" repeated Lucas, and she swung round to face him. Her eyes, of an unusually bright blue, were hostile. He was aware of emotion close to tumult; but she answered him clearly enough.

"I don't mind talking to her."

"She may say things that will distress you."

The fierce eyes narrowed. "What has she said about me?"

"Nothing. But she's mentally disturbed."

"Mad, you mean?"

"Schizoid, certainly. I think she's coming out of a period of disjunction. She may have suffered some extreme shock, that's recalled earlier trauma, perhaps the death of her mother. If she is in love with your husband, then meeting you may serve as a focus; bring her back to the present, in a sense." As Christine offered no comment, Lucas went on, "If you can hold her attention for five or ten minutes, Captain Finlander will use that time to get a net spread across the road, underneath the balcony."

"All right. What do I do?"

"When the moment seems right, go out there. Don't move quickly, or go close to her...."

"She's dangerous?"

"She's dangerous to herself," said Lucas gently.

Again Christine turned to look at Arnold. He seemed to be deep in conversation with Marion Dykes. Finlander, who had been waiting silently at the foot of the stairway, now said in an urgent voice, "Mrs Kuper, we must hurry."

"All right."

She squared her shoulders and without another glance at either of her companions, started up the stairs. At that moment, the woman on the balcony broke into sudden screaming.

"David? David? David?"

There was hysteria in the sound, but there was also a terrible entreaty. Christine Kuper sprang up the last few steps and crossed the gallery to the open doors. She saw a burly man rising to his feet, and beyond him, on the ledge, a girl half-crouched, head thrown back, like an animal baying the moon.

Christine shouted, "Stop that! Stop that noise!"

The girl's head snapped round. The screaming ceased. Christine moved out onto the balcony.

"I'm David's wife," she said. "I want to talk to you."

46

BRONSON HURRIED INTO the stock-room and spoke to Coggin.

"Finlander says you're to go ahead, right now."

Coggin nodded and turned to the men at the windows. "All set?" he slipped a pencil torch from his jacket and moved to the central embrasure; flicked the light on and off twice. On the far side of the street, a hand lifted briefly above the warehouse balustrade.

Coggin picked up his own crossbow.

"Steady. Take aim. Fire!"

There was a hissing sound, like that of a rocket's ascent. The four lines snaked across darkness, arched over the warehouse roof, dropped, began to slide. They were snatched up by unseen hands, and drawn in. The slack lessened.

Coggin said quietly, "Pay out the net."

The four men leaned over and freed the careful folds; slowly, silently, like an anemone opening in deep water, the net spread, first sagging at a steep angle and then rising to tautness. Flakes of snow touched it.

There came a flicker of movement on the warehouse as a soldier dodged round one of the chimney stacks. Then a pause.

Bronson muttered, "Why are they waiting?"

"They're making the ropes fast."

At last two hands signalled in a boxer's handshake. "Okay," said Coggin. "It's secured."

The net was hardly visible except where snow clung momentarily to its strands. Coggin said, "Stay at your posts. If the girl falls, steady the stays, but don't jerk on them. I'll go out and bring her in. If I need help, Munro will follow me, okay Joe? But take it slow, that net's gonna buck. And the girl's crazy. If she fights, give her a chop or she'll have us all over."

"Right, Sarge."

They waited. There was no light now in the street below, none in the cafés and shops. The neon signs had been doused. The only illumination came from the balcony over their heads, that shone on the warehouse and the thinly-falling snow.

Coggin swung himself out to stand on the middle window-ledge. He stood with head lifted, listening for any sound that might give him warning of the girl's fall. He closed his mind to the chasm at his feet and the bitter cold of the air. He concentrated on the girl, on the net, on being ready to launch himself outwards with exactly the right amount of force.

For the first time that night, Death was confronted by a fellow professional.

47

QUINCEY AND TARBOTEN skirted the Yacht Basin and approached Gregg's Boathouse. There were few craft in the water at this time of the year, most of them being laid up for the winter. Three cars parked on the quay showed a sparkling skin of snow.

Commander Gregg, the owner, lived in a shack next to the boathouse. He answered the door briskly, a rubicund man in slacks and heavy pullover.

Quincey explained about Ella Rannault. Gregg cut him short. "Yes, yes. It was on television not so long ago. But how can I help?"

"Miss Rannault has a close friend, a Mr David Kuper. I understand Mr Kuper leases a garage from you?"

"That's correct."

"We're anxious to get in touch with Mr Kuper, sir. We'd like to check if his car's here."

"I don't think I'm entitled ..." began Gregg, and then stopped. "Bloody urgent, is it?"

"Yes, sir."

"Then we'll skip the frills. Come inside."

They waited in a scrupulously neat living-room while Gregg fetched a key from a small wall-safe. Then they left the shack by the kitchen door and crossed the big yard behind. This was bounded on three sides by sheds converted into garages with modern tip-up doors. Gregg unlocked one of these, opened it, reached inside and pressed a switch. He stepped inside, inviting the others to follow.

"Car's still here, anyway." He approached the white MG saloon and bent to the window. "Oh, my Christ!"

As Gregg reached for the car door, Tarboten thrust him aside and took his place.

The body of a man had been crammed into the space between the dashboard and the seat. His feet were tangled with the pedals, his back was arched round the gear-lever, his chin sagged on his chest. His right eye rolled upward in seeming enquiry and his left eye and the left half of his forehead had been crushed inward.

Tarboten straightened up. "Is it Kuper?"

"Yes." Gregg wiped a hand down his face. "He's stiff. He's been dead for hours. He must have been lying here all day."

Quincey, over on the other side of the car, stooped and came up with something in his grasp; a raffia shopping-basket containing fresh vegetables, some canned fruit and a bottle of apricot brandy.

48

THE MAN IN the grey overcoat ignored the attentions of Deryk Booth and marched across to Arnold.

"Mr Kuper? I'm Emil Rannault."

"Yes, thank God you're here. Your daughter is still on the ledge. Miss Dykes will take you up there...."

"I'm not able to do anything about that."

As Arnold's face slackened in shock, Rannault tugged off heavy gloves and stuffed them into a pocket. He had a grey, pocked skin, thick glasses, a mouth at once fleshy and snappish. "It's no use being unrealistic. I've not seen Ella for twelve years. She was removed from my care after she had attacked me with a knife. She has been three times in mental hospitals, and even in her sane periods, I am anathema to her. She hates me. Nothing I could do or say now, would be any help. I'm here on another matter."

Arnold struggled to find words. "Do you realise ... there are people trying to save her life ... perhaps at great risk to themselves?"

"We each of us take the risks we consider worthwhile. We take them to secure what we value. I value my position as a Government adviser, and you, I am sure, value your shop. I am here to protect both your interests, and mine." He glanced over his shoulder at Booth, who was standing nearby with Elaine Bondi and Miss Dykes. "You may prefer to hear me in private?"

"I have no secrets from my colleagues."

"Praiseworthy." Cold eyes studied Marion Dykes. "Your confidence in this lady I can appreciate. I hear nothing but good of her. I have been forced, during recent months, to ask a great many questions about the Kuper holdings. Forgive my bluntness, madam, but I can say I would count myself lucky to have you in my employ." He turned back to Arnold. "May I sit down?"

"Please." Arnold indicated a chair. Rannault sat. The three others, after a brief hesitation, joined the circle. Rannault seemed to have become convener of some grotesque meeting.

"I have watched the situation here," he said, "since last August. So I can say I know your business position pretty well. You have a family concern, which of course is subject to inbuilt dangers. Nature seldom uses the same mould twice, son seldom fits comfortably into father's shoes. Your son, by what I learn, has neither your judgement nor your application, although he is ambitious. He is anxious to take over from you. He feels you are no longer competent to run Kuper's. You on the other hand feel he is not yet ready to take over control. You block his aspirations. This has created the first and greatest of Kuper's difficulties. The second is purely geographic. Your store was built in 1933, on too small a piece of ground. A multi-storey selling-area has serious drawbacks. You badly need to extend, but the only piece of proximate land is the Mission site. To my knowledge, your firm has made three offers for it in recent years, all of them being refused. Five months ago, there was another approach. Did you know this?"

Arnold pressed a hand to his chest. "I did not initiate such a move."

"Did you not?" Rannault's glance shifted to Booth. "Then this gentleman acted without your knowledge?"

Arnold said nothing. Rannault spread thick fingers. "Well, it happens. He approached my lawyers, on behalf of a consortium of buyers, he said. He was told the land was not for sale. No doubt he will tell you he was merely flying a kite. I leave it to you to decide whether his action was in line with the Companies Act, or his own conditions of service. I merely tell you that the approach was reported to me, as are all such attempts to obtain possession of shares or property belonging to my daughter."

"Your ... ?"

"My daughter. Ella is the major shareholder in the Mission property. The shares passed to her in her mother's estate. I'm glad to think you at least are ignorant of the fact."

"Mr Rannault, why are you telling me these things?"

"I am coming to the point. After I learnt of Mr Booth's offer, I was sufficiently alert to try and discover what funds were backing him. It was easy enough to determine that he could not be meeting the price himself. It took a rather longer time to establish that the money comes from the company controlling the Sizzle Discount Stores. I understand that you have been resisting a move to amalgamate Kuper's with Sizzle. Apparently neither Mr Booth, nor your son, shares your opinion on this. Quite clearly, they are already working very closely with Sizzle's principals."

"May I ask how you obtained this ... dubious information?"

"I bought it. I am very rich, and I have no scruples in how I deal with people who try to take unfair advantage of me."

Booth tried to intervene, but Arnold signed him to silence. "Later, Deryk. Mr Rannault, if you wish to see your daughter, I will take you to her. If not, then I ask you to leave."

"I am not yet ready to leave. I did not fly this distance, in a snowstorm, to exchange civilities. I have an important position in Governmental and financial circles. Scandal would damage me, so I prefer to settle things quietly. But I give you notice that if I am driven to it, I will take public action against your son, Mr Kuper."

"David has done nothing actionable."

"Don't let us quibble over words. He has driven Ella

to a suicide attempt. Whatever her feelings for me, or mine for her, she is my daughter. I will not allow her to be exploited for gain. Your son entered into a liaison with her, for the sole purpose of getting her to sell him, or give him, her shares in the Mission property. I have a reputation for hard dealing, I know, but I have never contemplated seducing a woman with the mind of a sick child, in order to make my profits."

"You have no proof ... no shred of proof ... that David intended such a thing."

"Oh, but I do. I spoke to Ella about it, late last night. I found her quite ... elated. It seems your son told her he was prepared to leave his wife. Obtain a divorce. Marry Ella. She would bring a handsome dowry, you'll agree; large enough, apparently, to gild the pill of her mental instability."

Arnold looked like a man who is bleeding to death. He said, "You could have prevented such a marriage."

"How? Declared Ella's insanity, in a blaze of publicity? I told you, I protect what I value. I do not relish scandal. I took what steps I thought necessary. Unfortunately, they don't seem to have turned out well from Ella's point of view. No doubt the disappointment she feels has led to this little drama tonight. But don't worry. She's threatened suicide so often ... it's a weapon she uses, to get what she wants...."

"What did you do?" Arnold got to his feet and stood gripping the back of his chair. "What in God's name did you do?"

"Very simple. This morning early I telephoned Mrs Kuper. I told her precisely what David was planning. I pointed out that unless she wished to see her family involved in a most unpleasant legal fight, she must at once put an end to your son's activities. It seems clear that she has done so."

49

TARBOTEN HAD CALLED the Murder Squad, and spoken to Finlander. He now returned to the garage. He found Quincey and Gregg in the doorway of a large lean-to at the back.

"He was slugged in here," said Quincey. "There's extensive spread of blood and matter, so there must have been several blows. Weapon probably that mallet." He indicated an iron-headed hammer lying on the floor. "There's no lock on this door."

The lean-to was for storing boats. There was a hull on a cradle at one side, and a dinghy slung from the roof. A window in the far wall stood open. Tarboten picked his way across to it and glanced out.

"Six foot drop to the lane," he said.

"But nobody could get in that way," said Gregg. "The windows are always bolted."

"Not in," said Quincey. "Out."

Tarboten nodded. "Slugged in here, from the front. Dragged through to the garage and shoved into the car."

Gregg was still puzzled. "Why would anyone leave by the window? Why not by the door? Yard's pretty empty, this time of year." He caught the exchange of glances between the policemen. "You mean, because his clothes would be messed up?"

"Yes," said Tarboten. "You hit a person once, there may not be much blood. Hit him several times and there'll be plenty. Someone hit that guy often enough to spatter the wall. That person is going to be marked, too."

"He could have put on an oilskin," said Gregg.

"Was there one here?"

"Almost certainly." Gregg indicated a row of pegs on the garage wall. A couple of old windcheaters hung there.

Quincey said, "How many keys are there to this garage?"

"Three." Gregg was positive now. "My own, kept in the safe for emergencies, like tonight. The killer wouldn't come in and borrow that, would he? Then David ... Mr

Kuper ... had his own. I suppose that's in his pocket."
"We'll check when we can move him. And the third?"
"That was a reserve, given to Mrs Kuper."
"His wife?"
"No. His mother. She's a keen sailor, uses the boats quite a bit."
"Would you have her address, sir? And the wife's?"
"Yes. My God. I suppose you have to tell them ... ?"
"Yes, we do. It helps if there's a friend."
Gregg swallowed. "Well, I'm not close to them, you know. But I'll help if I'm needed."
"That's good of you, sir." Tarboten turned his head as a siren wailed further along Whytewych. "That's the boys coming. I'd like to use your 'phone again, if I may?"
"Of course."
Gregg accompanied the policeman across the yard. As they entered the house, a thought struck him. "That shopping basket, it's a woman's. Do you think a woman could have ... done that?"
Tarboten did not answer. A woman could have swung the mallet, even a frail woman; but it would take muscle to haul a dead or dying man from the lean-to to the car, and drag him into it. There was also the question of who closed the garage door, though now wasn't the time to ask questions. Except about Ella Rannault's clothing.
He had to 'phone the Captain.

"She's wearing a fur coat," said Finlander. "Karakul. Bought it at this store, just before closing-time this afternoon."
"And under that?"
"A tweed suit. Pink and grey. Man-tailored."
"That's what she was dressed in when she left home this morning. Kuper was killed by repeated, heavy blows. There's blood spattered right across one wall. The killer must have been marked."
"She could have put something over herself before she did it."

"I don't think so. This wasn't a premeditated crime, sir. Someone just lashed out at him. And that girl's been walking round a brightly-lit store in a pale-coloured suit all afternoon, and nobody saw any blood on her."

"You're right. There's no time ... I'll ring you back."

"What about Mrs Kuper? Do we take her in?"

There was no answer. Tarboten jiggled the cradle, but the line was dead.

50

DEIRDRE KUPER AND Paul November had moved to the small study at the back of the house, and sat now on opposite sides of the hearth. The television set flickered in its corner, but gave them nothing they wanted. Outside the snow grew thicker and the city fell silent.

Paul said suddenly, "did David have a garage in Whytewych?"

"What?"

"His garage at home is empty. I checked. But if he has another, somewhere ... ?"

"Yes, he does. It's down at Gregg's Boathouse."

"Is there a spare key?"

"Yes."

"Where?"

"In that desk."

"Get it, will you?" Paul had risen to his feet.

She stared up at him without moving. Her face was haggard, all colour wiped away by the strain of the night. She said foolishly, "You promised you wouldn't leave me alone."

"Get the key, Deirdre."

She went to the desk in the corner, opened the flap and pulled out an interior drawer. She rummaged through it and then turned the contents out onto the writing pad.

"It's not here."

Paul came to stand beside her. His fingers closed on her shoulder. "Find it."

Her eyes shone up at him, brilliant with animal fear. Without a word she sank down onto the chair before the desk and began to search through every shelf and drawer.

"It's not here."

"Who else knows where it's kept?"

"David. Christine. Arnold." She put a hand on his wrist, gripping it fiercely. "You think he's dead, don't you?"

Before he could answer her, the telephone in the hall started to ring.

51

NEITHER OF THE two women on the balcony had noticed the net spread beneath them. They were in a closed world, aware of nothing except each other. Lockval, standing in the shadow of a column, watched his chance to jump.

Ella Rannault was talking. She swayed a little from side to side and the words poured out, ceaseless yet disjointed, as if the mind that produced them was shuttering like a broken lens.

"I am his wife," she told Christine. "Not you not you. He said, 'She is no wife to me she is nothing nothing left.' He does not love you. I would ask and he would say Ella it is you my darling. He . . . does . . . not . . . love . . . you. That is true. Can you hear? His words. Ella my darling."

Her head dropped back, the scything of her body became more violent. She seemed to be trying to escape some demonic chorus. "Davey? I won't go in there. I won't look. Davey?"

Christine spoke. "He doesn't love anyone. All these months, while he's been making love to you, he has slept with me. You don't mean any more to him than I do. Neither of us means anything. He cheated Arnold. His own father."

The girl was not listening. Her eyes were as deep and dark as the sky, they were like holes through which eternity showed.

"White. Like sleep. A place to drink silence. That's what he told me."

Christine laughed. "Oh yes, it was one of his best phrases. So he took you to the shack? My shack. And did you admire the carving on my bedhead? Snow-eagles. Did you notice? Do you remember the feel of the rugs on the floor by the fire? Did you lie there naked with him? Did he tell you, 'Ella my darling, all I want in the world is you and the Mission land?' "

There was a scurry of movement down on the show-room floor. Christine ignored it, edging towards the figure on the ledge who moaned and swayed and spread thin arms to the sky.

"You helped him, you bitch. You helped him to cheat me, you helped him to cheat Arnold. But you lost out, didn't you? Davey isn't going to get the store and Davey isn't going to marry you, because Davey's dead. Isn't he, Ella my darling? Davey's dead."

Footsteps raced up the stairs, someone was shouting to Lockval, "Grab Mrs Kuper." The girl on the ledge screamed as Christine reached for her.

Lockval's spring was just too late. He saw the women grapple with each other, hands clawing and feet scrabbling for purchase on the icy stone. Ella Rannault lost her balance and lurched backwards, dragging Christine after her. Like some bizarre acrobatic turn the two figures cart-wheeled into space.

52

"I HEARD THEM yell," said Coggin, "and then they hit the net. One of them bounced and landed again on the same spot, but the other one ... she started to roll towards the edge."

He was standing in the show-room with Finlander. Lockval was there too, and a group of men over by the elevators. Milner had gone down to the street at once, but now that the ambulance had wailed away, he would be back.

Coggin pulled deeply on his cigarette.

"Was the doctor with the girl?"

"Yes. He'll see her admitted to the Werner."

"Will she recover?"

"I don't know. Lucas is a good man."

"And old Kuper?"

"Miss Dykes took him home."

"Poor sod."

"Yes." Finlander spoke patiently, waiting for Coggin's hands to stop shaking. "After they hit the net, what did you do?"

"Oh ... I yelled to them to keep still and hang on. The one in the middle was lying face down. I could see her fur coat, not her face. She was moaning. The other one was right on the edge, and the net was sagging badly with her weight.

"I told Munro to follow me and get the girl closest to us. I lay flat and slid forward slowly. I passed the first girl and waited while Munro got her back to the window. She didn't give any trouble, but pulling her in made the net buck. I didn't dare move.

"Soon as I could, I started forward again. The one at the edge was lying still. She was hanging onto the net with both hands. When I was about a foot away from her, someone on the balcony shouted, 'Watch it, Sergeant, she's a killer.'

"That phased me. I stopped moving. She turned her head and looked at me, and she said quite calmly, 'It's all right. I'm coming.' And then she said, 'Move back, please. Balance the net for me.'

"I didn't know if I could trust her. But she was right about the net. It was dangerous, with both our weights on the one side. So I shifted back, towards the middle. The net stopped swinging and I said, 'Okay. Move now.' And she did. She just kind of ... rolled over the edge. There was nothing I could do about it. She just ... went."

Coggin fell silent. After a moment he looked up. "Can I go now? I have to get the trucks packed up again, and up to the mountains. If I leave it much later, the roads'll be blocked."

Finlander nodded. "Yes, sure. We'll get in touch with you tomorrow, if need be. I'm grateful for what you did, you and your men. Without you, they'd both be dead."

"Yeah." Coggin was pulling on his beret, tweaking his tunic into position, drawing round himself the cloak of Army discipline. "Okay then, Captain. See you."

He walked briskly away.

Lockval looked at Finlander. "Was there a case against her?"

"Yes, and no. We have some facts. For instance that David Kuper was cheating on his wife, and that he was double-crossing his old man about the store. Emil Rannault found him out on both counts and tipped off the wife. We may be able to prove he 'phoned Christine Kuper this morning. Then there's a stretch that's mere conjecture.

"My guess is that Kuper did reach an agreement with the Rannault girl. Perhaps he promised to get a divorce and marry her. The morning of the murder, I'd say she was up first, wrote some message on the mirror, something quite harmless but personal, that he wouldn't want old Ma Samuels to read. Then she went off to do her shopping, and by mistake she took his ring of keys with her.

"Later on, he woke. Read the message and cleaned it off. Bathed, shaved, dressed. Was ready to go and found he had no key-ring. He waited a while, hoping Ella would be back, but for some reason her shopping took longer than usual. So finally, he rang his wife and asked her to bring him spares for the garage and the car ignition.

"He picked a fatal moment. Christine Kuper had spoken to Emil Rannault. She'd had enough time to work out what David's actions were going to mean to her and to Arnold Kuper.

"She got the spare keys and drove down to Whytewych, parked her car in the lane behind Gregg's Boatyard, and walked round and let herself into the garage. The yard was deserted, no one saw her go in. Kuper arrived soon after. I'd say there was a scene; she slugged him. Having killed him, she panicked, and stowed his body in the car, probably meaning to drive it away and stash it somewhere. But at that point she heard someone coming across the yard. Ella Rannault, having found David's keys in her bag, had decided to come down to the garage and wait for him there.

"Mrs Kuper couldn't do anything but retreat into the lean-to shed and close the door. Ella Rannault entered the garage, looked into the car and saw Kuper's body. According to Dr Lucas, seeing him like that, lying in the white MG and covered in blood, could easily have jerked her mind back to the worst thing that ever happened to her ... finding her mother dead in the bath, with her wrists cut.

"Lucas thinks she reacted by going into amnesic shock. Her mind blotted out what she'd seen. She dropped the shopping basket she was carrying, ran out of the garage and slammed it shut. It has an automatic lock. Then she probably wandered about aimlessly, the same way an accident victim can do. About three o'clock, she called at her bank and cashed a cheque for two thousand. She came up to Kuper's and spent most of the money. She was still trying to black out the truth. She wanted to believe Kuper was alive. She bought him a lot of Christmas presents and had them wrapped. But by evening, the shock was wearing off. She began to realise he was dead. She began to think about the last trick in the bag, one she'd used before to make people rally round when she was desperate. She would threaten to kill herself; people would come, David would come, everything would be all right again. She got out on the balcony.

"She told the men who found her that when it started to snow, she'd jump. Lucas says, in her mind, white and death are closely connected.

"Mrs Kuper, meanwhile, did the only thing she could.

She was locked in the garage with a body, so she opened the window of the shed, dropped to the lane, and reached her car. Drove home. No doubt she made some attempt to clean up the clothes she was wearing, or dispose of them; but she was an intelligent woman. Must have known that sort of action would tell against her. She wasn't the one to face life imprisonment, so she jumped."

He looked at Milner. "Have they moved her?"

"Yes. The street's clear. Nothing more for them to see."

"We'd better get down to Whytewych, then. Locky, will you see to those doors?"

Finlander handed over the bunch of keys with its turquoise amulet. Lockval climbed the staircase.

He stood for a moment looking out at the ledge, empty against a backdrop of steadily-falling snow. The girl's father had flown back to the coast without even going near her.

He pulled the doors shut and turned the key.

53

PAUL NOVEMBER WAITED for Marion Dykes to reach the hallway before he spoke.

"Is she asleep?"

"No. She won't take anything. She wants to be awake if Arnold needs her."

"Can I give you a lift home?"

"No, I think I'll stay. The nurse can't deal with the Press, or ... or personal things. I'd rather be here myself."

"Will you give Mrs Kuper a message from me? Say I'll be round first thing in the morning?"

"I'll tell her. Thank you."

The Spanfexa clock registered midnight.

For a few seconds it seemed to remain with hands folded for the passing of the day; then movement, change, tomorrow.

Traffic flowed in Manning Lane, the shops glittered on

Parade Square, the cafés and restaurants overflowed. In the centre of the area a team of men struggled to raise a fifty-foot Christmas tree, urged on by a shouting, singing mob.

Paul, halted at a traffic-light, saw the crowd and hated it, because it danced and rejoiced while he grieved. Yet his anger, like his grief, tied him to these people. They were alive, as he was, and part of the same pilgrimage.

You can say that in any city, at any season, Death will find his boon companions. He's a good talker. But then, so is Life. Statistics show that in their dealings with ordinary mortals, both Death and Life have one hundred per cent success.